LearningCurve activity is available for this topic. Visit **bedfordstmartins.com/rwinteractive.**

Real
Writing
INTERACTIVE

A Brief Guide to Writing
Paragraphs and Essays

Susan Anker

Bedford / St. Martin's
Boston ◆ New York

For Bedford/St. Martin's

Publisher for College Success and Developmental Studies: Edwin Hill
Executive Editor for Developmental Studies: Alexis Walker
Developmental Editor: Jill Gallagher
Senior Production Editor: Bridget Leahy
Senior Production Supervisor: Dennis Conroy
Marketing Manager: Christina Shea
Copy Editor: Steve Patterson
Indexer: Melanie Belkin
Senior Art Director: Anna Palchik
Text Design: Claire Seng-Niemoller
Cover Design: Billy Boardman
Composition: Graphic World Inc.
Printing and Binding: RR Donnelley and Sons

President, Bedford/St. Martin's: Denise B. Wydra
Editorial Director for English and Music: Karen S. Henry
Director of Development: Erica T. Appel
Director of Marketing: Karen R. Soeltz
Production Director: Susan W. Brown
Director of Rights and Permissions: Hilary Newman

Manufactured in the United States of America.

8   7   6   5   4   3
f   e   d   c   b   a

For information, write: Bedford/St. Martin's, 75 Arlington Street, Boston, MA 02116   (617-399-4000)

ISBN 978-1-4576-5411-4

Acknowledgments

Acknowledgments and copyrights can be found at the back of the book on page 239, which constitutes an extension of the copyright page. It is a violation of the law to reproduce these selections by any means whatsoever without the written permission of the copyright holder.

Contents

Part Two
Writing Different Kinds of Paragraphs and Essays

Preface

Real Writing Interactive has a two-fold goal: to show students that writing is essential to success in the real world and to help them develop the skills they need to achieve that success in their own college, work, and everyday lives. In support of this message, the book provides both an engaging real-world context for writing, and exercises and activities that will help students write strong paragraphs and essays—all in a brief, affordable format.

Real Writing Interactive (like *Real Skills Interactive* and *Real Essays Interactive*) reframes writing for students who view it as irrelevant and impossible—instead it presents writing and the work of the writing class as eminently learnable and potentially life-altering, and therefore worthy of students' best efforts. *Real Writing Interactive* is written in a new interactive format that brings grammar practice to life via LearningCurve, a game-like, adaptive quizzing system that helps students learn as they go.

Core Features

■ **Brief, Affordable Format.** The text offers what's essential for the paragraph-to-essay level course—process-oriented writing instruction and focused grammar lessons—in a concise and affordable format.

■ ✓ **Interactive Grammar Practice via LearningCurve.** LearningCurve's innovative adaptive online quizzing lets students learn at their own pace, and a game-like interface encourages them to keep at it. Quizzes are keyed to grammar instruction in the book, so what is taught in class gets reinforced at home. Instructors can also check in on each student's activity in a grade book.

A student access code is printed in every new student copy of *Real Writing Interactive*. Students who do not buy a new print book or e-book can purchase access by going to **bedfordstmartins.com /rwinteractive**. Instructors can also get access at this site.

NOTE: LearningCurve is also available in WritingClass or SkillsClass, so if you're using either Class, encourage your students to use it there.

■ **Real-World Examples.** Samples of real students' writing demonstrate the concepts covered and give students confidence that good writing skills are achievable. These models address such real-world issues and concerns as answering challenging job interview questions and staying organized at work.

- **Four Basics Boxes.** Presenting writing skills in manageable increments, these boxes break down the essentials of topics such as revision, good paragraphs, and narration.

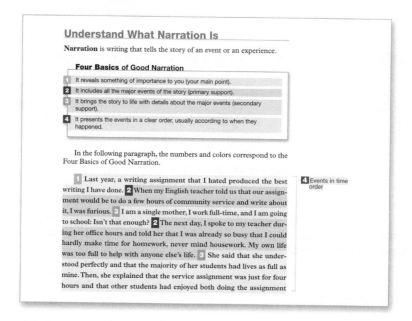

Understand What Narration Is

Narration is writing that tells the story of an event or an experience.

Four Basics of Good Narration

1. It reveals something of importance to you (your main point).
2. It includes all the major events of the story (primary support).
3. It brings the story to life with details about the major events (secondary support).
4. It presents the events in a clear order, usually according to when they happened.

In the following paragraph, the numbers and colors correspond to the Four Basics of Good Narration.

1 Last year, a writing assignment that I hated produced the best writing I have done. 2 When my English teacher told us that our assignment would be to do a few hours of community service and write about it, I was furious. 3 I am a single mother, I work full-time, and I am going to school: Isn't that enough? 2 The next day, I spoke to my teacher during her office hours and told her that I was already so busy that I could hardly make time for homework, never mind housework. My own life was too full to help with anyone else's life. 3 She said that she understood perfectly and that the majority of her students had lives as full as mine. Then, she explained that the service assignment was just for four hours and that other students had enjoyed both doing the assignment

4 Events in time order

- **Focus on the Four Most Serious Errors.** *Real Writing Interactive* concentrates first on the four types of grammatical errors that matter most: fragments, run-ons, errors in subject-verb agreement, and errors of verb tense and form, and helps students avoid making them. Once students master these four topics and start building their editing skills, they are better prepared to tackle the grammar errors treated in later chapters.

You Get More with *Real Writing Interactive*

Real Writing Interactive does not stop with a book. Online, you will find more resources to help students get even more out of the book and your course. You will also find free, convenient instructor resources, such as a downloadable instructor's manual.

For more information, visit **bedfordstmartins.com/rwinteractive /catalog**.

STUDENT RESOURCES

Premium Resources

- **WritingClass** provides students with a dynamic, interactive online course space preloaded with exercises, diagnostics, video tutorials, and more. WritingClass helps students stay focused and lets instructors see how they are progressing. It is available at a significant discount when packaged with the print text. To learn more about WritingClass, visit **yourwritingclass.com**.

- **SkillsClass** offers all that WritingClass offers, plus guidance and practice in reading and study skills. This interactive online course space comes preloaded with exercises, diagnostics, video tutorials, and more. It is available at a significant discount when packaged with the print text. To learn more about SkillsClass, visit **yourskillsclass.com**.

- *Re:Writing Plus,* **now with VideoCentral,** gathers all of our premium digital content for the writing class into one online collection. This impressive resource includes innovative and interactive help with writing a paragraph; tutorials and practices that show how writing works in students' real-world experience; VideoCentral, with more than 140 brief videos for the writing classroom; the first ever peer-review game, *Peer Factor*; plus hundreds of models of writing and hundreds of readings. *Re:Writing Plus* can be purchased separately or packaged with *Real Writing Interactive* at a significant discount.

Free* with the Print Text

- **The *Bedford/St. Martin's ESL Workbook*** includes a broad range of exercises covering grammatical issues for multilingual students of varying language skills and backgrounds. Answers are at the back. ISBN: 978-0-312-54034-0

- **The *Make-a-Paragraph Kit*** is a fun, interactive CD-ROM that teaches students about paragraph development. It also contains exercises to help students build their own paragraphs, audio-visual tutorials on four of the most common errors for basic writers, and the content from *Exercise Central to Go: Writing and Grammar Practices for Basic Writers*. ISBN: 978-0-312-45332-9

- **The *Bedford/St. Martin's Planner*** includes everything that students need to plan and use their time effectively, with advice on preparing schedules and to-do lists plus blank schedules and calendars (monthly and weekly). The planner fits easily into a backpack or purse, so students can take it anywhere. ISBN: 978-0-312-57447-5

    ***NOTE:* There is a limit of one free supplement per order.** Additional supplements can be packaged at a significant discount.

e-Book Options

Real Writing Interactive e-book. Available as a value-priced e-book, either as a CourseSmart e-book or in formats for use with computers, tablets, and e-readers—visit **bedfordstmartins.com/rwinteractive/catalog** for more information.

INSTRUCTOR RESOURCES

- *Practical Suggestions for Teaching Real Essays Interactive* provides helpful information and advice on teaching developmental writing. It includes sample syllabi, tips on building students' critical thinking skills, resources for teaching nonnative English speakers and speakers of nonstandard English dialects, ideas for assessing students' writing and progress, and up-to-date suggestions for using technology in the writing classroom and lab. To download, see **bedfordstmartins.com/rwinteractive/catalog**.

- *Additional Resources for Teaching Real Essays Interactive* is a collection of resources that supplements the instructional materials in the text. It contains a variety of extra exercises and tests, transparency masters, planning forms, and other reproducibles for classroom use. To download, see **bedfordstmartins.com/rwinteractive/catalog**.

- *Answer Key for Real Essays Interactive* contains answers to the practice exercises in the printed book. To download, see **bedfordstmartins.com/rwinteractive/catalog**.

Acknowledgments

As with the rest of the Anker series, *Real Writing Interactive* grew out of a collaboration with teachers and students across the country and with the talented staff of Bedford/St. Martin's. I am grateful for everyone's thoughtful contributions.

REVIEWERS

I would like to thank the following instructors for their many good ideas and suggestions for this edition. Their insights were invaluable.

Nikki Aitken, Illinois Central College
Valerie Badgett, Lon Morris College
Michael Briggs, East Tennessee State University
Andrew Cavanaugh, University of Maryland University College
Jeff Kosse, Iowa Western Community College
Mimi Leonard, Wytheville Community College

Shannon McCann, Suffolk Community College
Loren Mitchell, Hawaii Community College
Jim McKeown, McLennan Community College
Virginia Nugent, Miami Dade College
Lisa Oldaker Palmer, Quinsigamond Community College
Anne Marie Prendergast, Bergen Community College
Gina Schochenmaier, Iowa Western Community College
Karen Taylor, Belmont College
Elizabeth Wurz, College of Coastal Georgia
Svetlana Zhuravlova, Lakeland Community College

STUDENTS

Many current and former students have helped shape *Real Writing Interactive,* and I am grateful for all of their contributions.

Among the students who provided paragraphs and essays for the book are Jess Murphy, John Around Him, Shari Beck, Jasen Beverly, Charlton Brown, Dominic Deiro, Brian Healy, Kelly Hultgren, Said Ibrahim, Amanda Jacobowitz, Jelani Lynch, Lauren Mack, Lorenza Mattazi, Holly Moeller, Casandra Palmer, Robert Phansalkar, Caitlin Prokop, Dara Riesler, Heather Rushall, True Shields, Courtney Stoker, and Jason Yilmaz.

I would also like to thank the nine former students who provided inspirational words of advice and examples of workplace writing which are central to the book. They are Mary LaCue Booker, Jeremy Graham, Celia Hyde, Leigh King, Kelly Layland, Brad Leibov, Diane Melancon, Walter Scanlon, and Karen Upright.

A Note to Students from Susan Anker

For the last twenty years or so, I have traveled the country talking to students about their goals and, more important, about the challenges they face on the way to achieving those goals. Students always tell me that they want good jobs and that they need a college degree to get those jobs. I designed *Real Writing Interactive* with those goals in mind—strengthening the writing, reading, and editing skills needed for success in college, at work, and in everyday life.

Here is something else: Good jobs require not only a college degree but also a college education—knowing not only how to read and write but how to think critically and learn effectively. So that is what I stress here, too. It is worth facing the challenges. All my best wishes to you, in this course and in all your future endeavors.

Critical Thinking, Reading, and Writing

Making Connections

In order to become a better writer, you need to use critical thinking and reading skills. This chapter explains critical thinking and reading strategies and explores the important connections among critical thinking, reading, and writing.

Critical Thinking

You are already a critical thinker. If you have ever questioned a claim made by a politician or second-guessed an advertisement, you were thinking critically about what you saw, heard, or read.

Critical thinking is a process of actively questioning what you see, hear, and read to come to thoughtful conclusions about it. Critical thinking also involves making connections between existing impressions and new ones, and among various beliefs, claims, and pieces of information.

Four Basics of Critical Thinking

1. Be alert to assumptions made by you and others.
2. Question those assumptions.
3. Consider and connect various points of view — even those different from your own.
4. Keep an open mind and avoid hasty conclusions.

✓ LearningCurve For extra practice in the skills covered in this chapter, visit: bedfordstmartins.com/rwinteractive.

1

Assumptions—ideas or opinions that we do not question and that we automatically accept as true—can get in the way of clear, critical thinking. In college, work, and everyday life, we often make judgments based on assumptions that we are not even aware of. By identifying these assumptions and questioning them, we stand a better chance of seeing things as they are and responding to them more effectively.

When questioning assumptions, try to get a bit of distance from them. Imagine what people with entirely different points of view might say. You might even try disagreeing with your own assumptions. Take a look at the following examples.

Questioning Assumptions

SITUATION	ASSUMPTION	QUESTIONS
College: I saw from the syllabus that I need to write five essays for this course.	That sounds like too much work.	What obstacles might be getting in my way? What might be some ways around those obstacles? What have others done in this situation?
Work: Two of my coworkers just got raises.	My own raise is just around the corner.	Did my coworkers accomplish anything that I didn't? When was their last raise, and when was mine?
Everyday Life: My neighbor has been cool to me lately.	I must have done something wrong.	Is it possible that this has nothing to do with me? Maybe he is going through something difficult in his life?

You need to be aware not only of your own hidden assumptions but also of any assumptions hidden in what you read, see, and hear. For example, look at the bottled water label on page 3. Labels like this one might suggest directly or indirectly that bottled water is better than tap water. What evidence do they provide for this assumption? What other sources of information could be consulted to support, disprove, or call into question this assumption? However confidently a claim is made, never assume that it cannot be questioned.

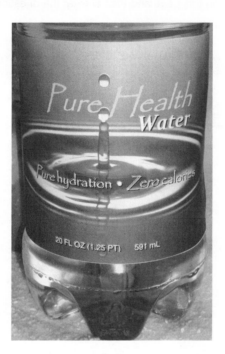

Label from a leading brand of bottled water

In addition to assumptions, be aware of **biases**, one-sided and sometimes prejudiced views that may blind you to the truth of any situation. Here is just one example:

Kids today don't read.

This is an extreme statement that others could contradict with their own experiences or additional information (for example, pointing out the success of the *Harry Potter* series, or giving examples of "kids" who *are* readers).

Be on the lookout for bias in your own views and in whatever you read, see, and hear. When a statement seems one-sided or extreme, ask yourself what facts or points of view might have been omitted.

PRACTICE 1 Thinking Critically

Look at the images on this page and then answer the questions that follow.

Advertisement from Tappening, a group that opposes bottled water

Label from a leading brand of bottled water

*Last year, plastic bottles generated more than 2.5 million tons of carbon dioxide. **Drink tap. tappening.com**

- What is the main message of the advertisement? What is the main message of the bottled water label?

- Make a connection between the two images: How are they alike? How are they different?

- What assumptions are behind each of the images? Write down as many as you can identify. Then, write down questions about these assumptions, considering different points of view.

- Which image do you find more effective? Why?

- Collaborate: Do others in your group agree with the way you "read" each image? Why or why not? What makes you read them the way you do?

Critical Reading

When you practice **critical reading**, you apply your critical thinking skills to your reading. To do this, you need to read actively, paying close attention to the text and asking yourself questions about the author's purpose, his or her main point, the support he or she gives, and how good that support is. It is important to think critically as you read, looking out for assumptions and biases (both the writer's and your own). You should also consider whether you agree or disagree with the points being made.

Here are the four steps of the critical reading process:

2PR   The Critical Reading Process

■ **Preview** the reading.

■ **Read** the piece, double underlining the <u>thesis statement</u> and underlining the <u>major support</u>. Consider the quality of the support.

■ **Pause** to think during the reading. Take notes and ask questions about what you are reading. Imagine that you are talking to the author.

■ **Review** the reading, your marginal notes, and your questions.

2PR   Preview the Reading

Before reading any piece of writing, skim the whole thing, using the following steps.

■ **Read the title, head note, and introductory paragraphs** to determine the topic and main point of the reading. Consider whether these elements give clues as to the purpose of and audience for the piece.

■ **Read headings, key words, and definitions** to help follow the author's main ideas and important concepts.

■ **Look for summaries, checklists, and chapter reviews** to make sure you understand the main points.

■ **Read the conclusion** to confirm the reading's main idea.

■ **Ask a guiding question**—a question you think the reading might answer—to help keep you focused as you read.

2PR   Read the Piece: Find the Main Point and the Support

After previewing, begin reading carefully for meaning, trying especially to identify the writer's main point and the support for that point.

MAIN POINT, PURPOSE, AND AUDIENCE

For more on main points, see pages 29–37.

The **main point** of a reading is the central idea the author wants to communicate. The main point is related to the writer's **purpose**, which can be to explain, to demonstrate, to persuade, or to entertain, and to his or her intended **audience**, which can range from specific (say, a particular person) to general (any reader of a periodical). Writers often introduce their main point early, so read the first few paragraphs with special care. If the writer has stated the main point in a single sentence, double-underline it.

SUPPORT

Support is the evidence that shows, explains, or proves the main point. The author might use statistics, facts, definitions, and scientific results for support, or he or she might use memories, stories, comparisons, quotations from experts, and personal observations.

For more on support, see pages 37–41.

Not all support is good support. When you are reading, ask yourself: What information is the author including to help me understand or agree with the main point? Is the support (evidence) valid and convincing? If not, why not?

Here's an example of a well-constructed paragraph. The main point is double-underlined, and the support is underlined.

Making a plan for your college studies is a good way to reach your academic goals. The first step to planning is answering this question: "What do I want to be?" If you have only a general idea—for example, "I would like to work in the health-care field"—break this large area into smaller, more specific subfields. These subfields might include working as a registered nurse, a nurse practitioner, or a physical therapist. The second step to planning is to meet with an academic adviser to talk about the classes you will need to take to get a degree or certificate in your chosen field. Then, map out the courses you will be taking over the next couple of semesters. Throughout the whole process, bear in mind the words of student mentor Ed Powell: "Those who fail to plan, plan to fail." A good plan boosts your chances of success in college and beyond.

PRACTICE 2   Finding the Main Point and Support

Read the following paragraph. Double-underline the main point and underline
the support.

> Networking is a way businesspeople build connections with others
> to get ahead. Building connections in college also is well worth the
> effort. One way to build connections is to get to know some of your
> classmates and to exchange names, phone numbers, and e-mail
> addresses with them. That way, if you cannot make it to a class, you
> will know someone who can tell you what you missed. You can also
> form study groups with these other students. Another way to build
> connections is to get to know your instructor. Make an appointment
> to visit your instructor during his or her office hours. When you
> go, ask questions about material you are not sure you understood
> in class or problems you have with other course material. You and
> your instructor will get the most out of these sessions if you bring
> examples of specific assignments that you are having trouble with.

2PR   Pause to Think

Taking notes and asking questions as you read will help you understand the
author's points and develop a thoughtful response. As you read:

- Double-underline the main idea or write it in the margin.
- Note the major support points by underlining them.
- Note ideas that you agree with by placing a check mark next to
  them (✓).
- Note ideas that you do not agree with or that surprise you with an
  X or !.
- Note ideas you do not understand with a question mark (?).
- Note any examples of an author's or expert's assumptions or biases.
- Jot any additional notes or questions in the margin.
- Consider how parts of the reading relate to the main point.

2PR   Review and Respond

After reading, take a few minutes to look back and review. Go over your
guiding question, your marginal notes, and your questions—and connect
with what you have read. Consider, "What interested me? What did I learn?
How does it fit with what I know from other sources?" When you have reviewed your reading in this way and fixed it well in your mind and memory,

For more
on writing
critically about
readings, see
pages 10–16.

it is much easier to respond in class discussion and writing. To write about a reading, you need to generate and organize your ideas, draft and revise your response, and above all, use your critical thinking skills.

A Critical Reader at Work

Read the following piece. The notes in the margin show how one student applied the process of critical reading to an essay on bottled water.

Amanda Jacobowitz

A Ban on Water Bottles: A Way to Bolster the University's Image

Amanda Jacobowitz is a student at Washington University and a columnist for the university's publication *Student Life,* in which the following essay appeared.

Guiding Question: What does the author think about the ban on bottled water?

Lately, I am always thirsty. Always! I could not figure out why 1 until I realized that the bottled water I had purchased continuously throughout my day had disappeared. At first I was just confused. Where did all the water bottles go? Then I learned the simple explanation: The University banned water bottles in an effort to be environmentally friendly.

Larger main point (not stated directly): (1) the ban is ineffective, and (2) there are better ways to protect the environment.

Why not just drink from a water fountain? You don't have to have a bottle.

Ideally, given the ban on selling water bottles, every student on 2 campus should now take the initiative to carry a water bottle, filling it up throughout the day at the water fountains on campus. Realistically, we know this has not and will not happen. I have tried to bring a water bottle with me to classes—I do consider myself somewhat environmentally conscious—but have rarely succeeded in this effort. Instead, although I have never been too much of a soda drinker, I find myself reaching for a bottle of Coke out of pure convenience. We can't buy bottled water, but we can buy soda, juice, and other

Examples of other common forms of waste

drinks, many of which come in plastic bottles. I am sure that for most people—particularly those who give very little thought to being environmentally conscientious—convenience prevails and they purchase a drink other than water. Wonderful result. The University can pride itself on being more environmentally friendly, with the fallback that its students will be less healthy!

3   Even if students are not buying unhealthy drinks, any benefit from the reduction of plastic water bottles could easily be offset by its alternatives. Students are not using their hands to drink water during meals. They are using plastic cups—cups provided by the University at every eatery on campus. Presumably no person picks up a cup, drinks their glass of water, and then saves that same cup for later in the day. That being said, how many plastic cups are used by a single student, in a single day? How many cups are used by the total campus-wide population daily, yearly? This plastic cup use must equate to an exorbitant amount of waste as well.

— *Examples of other common forms of waste*

4   My intent is not to have the University completely roll back the water bottle ban, nor is my intent for the University to level the playing field by banning all plastic drink bottles. I'm simply questioning the reasons for specifically banning bottled water of all things? Why not start with soda bottles—decreasing the environmental impact, as well as the health risks. There are also many other ways to help the environment that seem to be so easily overlooked.

— *Examples of other ways to protect the environment*

5   Have you ever noticed a patch of grass on campus that's not perfectly green? I can't say that I have. The reason: the sprinklers. Now, I admit that I harbor some animosity when it comes to the campus sprinklers; I somehow always manage to mistakenly and inadvertently walk right in their path, the spray of water generously dousing my feet. However, my real problem with the sprinklers is the waste of water they represent. Do we really need our grass to be green at all times?

6   The landscaping around our beloved Danforth University Center (Gold LEED Certified) is irrigated with the use of rainwater. There is a 50,000-gallon rainwater tank below the building to collect rain! I admit, this is pretty impressive, but what about the rest of the campus? What water is used to irrigate and keep green the rest of our 169 acres on the Danforth campus?

— *Town/city water, I assume.*

I understand that being environmentally conscious is difficult 7
to do, particularly at an institutional level. I applaud the Danforth
University Center and other environmental efforts the University
has initiated. However, I can't help but wonder if the University's
ban on the sale of water bottles is more about appearance and less
about decreasing the environmental impact of our student body.
The water bottle ban has become a way to build the school's public
image: we banned water bottles, we are working hard to be environmentally friendly! In reality, given the switch to plastic cups and
the switch to other drinks sold in plastic bottles, is the environmental impact of the ban that significant? Now that the ban has been
implemented, I certainly don't see the University retracting it.
Is it really about   However, I hope that in the future the University focuses less on its
public image?
What would —————   public image and more on the environment itself when instituting
a university
administrator   such dramatic changes.
say?

PRACTICE 3   Making Connections

Look back at the advertisement on page 4 and the bottled water labels
on pages 3 and 4. Then, review the reading by Amanda Jacobowitz. What
assumptions does Jacobowitz make about bottled water? What evidence, if
any, is provided to support these assumptions? Based on your observations,
would you like to see bottled water not banned or banned at your college? Why
or why not?

Writing Critically about Readings

There are different types of writing in college. In Chapters 2 through 4, we
examine the writing process in general and learn how to draft and revise
paragraphs and essays. In Chapters 5 through 13, we explore the different
techniques for developing an essay, such as narration and illustration.

In this section, we discuss the key college skill of writing critically about
what you read. In any college course, your instructor may ask you to summarize, analyze, synthesize, or evaluate one or more readings to demonstrate your deep understanding of the material. When you do so, you answer
the following questions.

Writing Critically

Summarize

- What is important about the text?
- What is the purpose, the big picture? Who is the intended audience?
- What are the main points and key support?

Analyze

- What elements have been used to convey the main point?
- Do any elements raise questions? Do any key points seem missing or undeveloped?

Synthesize

- What do other sources say about the topic of the text?
- How does your own (or others') experience affect how you see the topic?
- What new point(s) might you make by bringing together all the different sources and experiences?

Evaluate

- Based on your application of summary, analysis, and synthesis, what do you think about the material you have read?
- Is the work successful? Does it achieve its purpose?
- Does the author show any biases? Are there any hidden assumptions? If so, do they make the piece more or less effective?

Summary

A **summary** is a condensed, or shortened, version of something—often, a longer piece of writing, a movie or television show, a situation, or an event. In writing a summary, you give the main points and key support in your own words.

Following is an excerpt from the *Textbook of Basic Nursing* by Caroline Bunker Rosdahl and Mary T. Kowalski. It comes from a chapter that discusses some of the stresses that families can face, including divorce.

> Adults who are facing separation from their partners—and a return to single life—may feel overwhelmed. They may become preoccupied with their own feelings, thereby limiting their ability to handle the situation effectively or to be strong for their children.

The breakdown of the family system may require a restructuring of responsibilities, employment, childcare, and housing arrangements. Animosity between adults may expose children to uncontrolled emotions, arguments, anger, and depression.

Children may feel guilt and anxiety over their parents' divorce, believing the situation to be their fault. They may be unable to channel their conflicting emotions effectively. Their school performance may suffer, or they may engage in misbehavior. Even when a divorce is handled amicably, children may experience conflicts about their loyalties and may have difficulties making the transition from one household to another during visitation periods. . . .

Experts estimate that approximately 50% of all children whose parents divorce will experience another major life change within 3 years: remarriage. The arrival of a stepparent in the home presents additional stressors for children. Adapting to new rules of behavior, adjusting to a new person's habits, and sharing parents with new family members can cause resentment and anger. When families blend children, rivalries and competition for parental attention can lead to repeated conflicts.

Now, here is a summary of the textbook excerpt. The main point is double-underlined, and the support points are underlined.

Although divorce seriously affects the people who are splitting up, Rosdahl and Kowalski point out that the couple's children face equally difficult consequences, both immediately and in the longer term. In the short term, according to the authors, children may blame themselves for the split or feel that their loyalty to both parents is divided. These negative emotions can affect their behavior at school and elsewhere. Later on, if one or both of the parents remarry, the children may have trouble adjusting to the new family structure.

A summary is a useful way to record information from a reading in a course notebook. You can put the main points of an article into your own words for later review. You may also be asked to provide summaries in homework assignments or on tests in order to show that you read and understood a reading. In addition, summary is an important tool for keeping track of information for a research project.

Analysis

An **analysis** breaks down the points or parts of something and considers how they work together to make an impression or convey a main point. When writing an analysis, you might also consider points or parts that seem to be missing or that raise questions in your mind. Your analysis of a reading provides the main points as well as your own reaction to the piece.

Here is an analysis of the excerpt from the *Textbook of Basic Nursing* on pages 11–12. The main point is double-underlined, and the support points are underlined.

> We all know that divorce is difficult for the people who are splitting up, but Rosdahl and Kowalski pay special attention to the problems faced by children of divorce, both right after the split and later on. The authors mention several possible outcomes of divorce on children, including emotional and behavioral difficulties and trouble in school. They also discuss the stresses that remarriage can create for children.
>
> The authors rightly emphasize the negative effects that divorce can have on children. However, I found myself wondering what a divorcing couple could do to help their children through the process. Also, how might parents and stepparents help children adjust to a remarriage? I would like to examine these questions in a future paper.

In any college course, your instructor may ask you to write an analysis to show your critical thinking skills and your ability to respond to a reading.

Synthesis

A **synthesis** pulls together information from additional sources or experiences to make a new point. Here is a synthesis of the textbook material on divorce (pp. 11–12). Because the writer wanted to address some of the questions she raised in her analysis, she incorporated additional details from published sources and from people she interviewed. Her synthesis of this information helped her arrive at a fresh conclusion.

> In the *Textbook of Basic Nursing*, Rosdahl and Kowalski focus on the   First source
> problems faced by children of divorce, both right after the split and later on. According to the authors, immediate problems can include emotional and behavioral difficulties and trouble in school. Later on, parents' marriage can create additional stresses for children. Although the authors discuss the impact of divorce on all parties, they do not suggest ways in which parents or stepparents might help children through the process of divorce or remarriage. However, other sources, as well as original research on friends who have experienced divorce as children or adults, provide some additional insights into these questions.

Second
source

A Web site produced by the staff at the Mayo Clinic recommends that parents come together to break the news about their divorce to their children. The Web site also suggests that parents keep the discussion brief and free of "ugly details." In addition, parents should emphasize that the children are in no way to blame for the divorce and that they are deeply loved. As the divorce proceeds, neither parent should speak negatively about the other parent in the child's presence or otherwise try to turn the child against the ex-spouse. Finally, parents should consider counseling for themselves or their children if any problems around the divorce persist.

Third source

The Web site of the University of Missouri Extension addresses the problems that can arise for children after their parents remarry. Specifically, the Web site describes several things that stepparents can do to make their stepchildren feel more comfortable with them and the new family situation. One strategy is to try to establish a friendship with the children before assuming the role of a parent. Later, once stepparents have assumed a more parental role, they should make sure they and their spouse stand by the same household rules and means of discipline. With time, the stepparents might also add new traditions for holidays and other family gatherings to help build new family bonds while respecting the old ones.

Fourth source

To these sources, I added interviews with three friends—two who are children of divorce and one who is both a divorced parent and a stepparent. The children of divorce said that they experienced many of the same difficulties and stresses that Rosdahl and Kowalski described. Interestingly, though, they also reported that they felt guilty, even though their parents told them not to, just as the Mayo Clinic experts recommend. As my friend Kris said, "For a long time after the divorce, every time me and my dad were together, he seemed distracted, like he wished I wasn't there. I felt bad that I couldn't just vanish." Dale, the stepparent I interviewed, liked the strategies suggested by the University of Missouri Extension, and he had actually tried some of these approaches with his own stepchildren. However, as Dale told me, "When you're as busy as most parents and kids are these days, you can let important things fall by the wayside—even time together. That's not good for anyone."

Fresh
conclusion

Thinking back on Kris's and Dale's words and everything I've learned from the other sources, I have come to conclude that divorced parents and stepparents need to make sure they build "together time" with their own children and/or stepchildren into every day. Even if this time is just a discussion over a meal or a quick bedtime story, children will remember it and appreciate it. This approach would help with some of the relationship building that the University of Missouri Extension recommends. It would also improve communication, help children understand that they are truly loved by *all* their parents, and assist with the process of postdivorce healing.

Works Cited

Leigh, Sharon and Maridith Jackson. "Foundations for a Successful Stepfamily." The University of Missouri Extension, Apr. 2007. Web. 13 Oct. 2011.

Mayo Clinic Staff. "Children and Divorce: Helping Kids After a Breakup." *Mayo Clinic*. The Mayo Clinic, 14 May 2011. Web. 12 Oct. 2011.

Rosdahl, Caroline Bunker, and Mary T. Kowalski. *Textbook of Basic Nursing.* 9th ed. Philadelphia: Lippincott Williams & Wilkins, 2008. 92. Print.

Synthesizing is important for longer writing assignments and research papers, in which you need to make connections among different works. Many courses that involve writing, such as history and psychology, require papers that synthesize information from more than one source.

Evaluation

An **evaluation** is your *thoughtful* judgment about something based on what you have discovered through your summary, analysis, and synthesis. To evaluate something effectively, apply the questions from the Writing Critically box on page 11. Here is an evaluation of the excerpt from the *Textbook of Basic Nursing* on pages 11–12.

> In just a few paragraphs, Rosdahl and Kowalski give a good description of the effects of divorce, not only on the former spouses but also on their children. The details that the authors provide help to clearly communicate the difficulties that such children face. In the short term, these difficulties can include emotional and behavioral problems and trouble in school. In the longer term, if one or both of a child's parents remarry, the child faces the stress of dealing with a new and different family. Although the authors do not specifically address ways that parents and stepparents can ease children into divorce and/or new families, other sources—such as the Web sites of the University of Missouri Extension and the Mayo Clinic, as well as people I interviewed—do get into these issues. In the end, I think that Rosdahl and Kowalski present a good overview of their subject in a short piece of writing that was part of a larger discussion on family stresses.

When you do college-level work, you must be able to evaluate the readings and other sources you encounter. Instructors may ask you to write evaluations in order to demonstrate your ability to question and judge sources.

PRACTICE 4   Making Connections

As you work through this exercise, refer to the Writing Critically box on page 11 and to your responses to Practice 3 (if you completed it).

1. **Summary:** Summarize Amanda Jacobowitz's essay on pages 8-10.

2. **Analysis:** Write a paragraph analyzing the points Jacobowitz presents.

3. **Synthesis:** Read additional opinion pieces or blog postings on bottled water. In one paragraph, state your position on the subject according to your reading of these materials. Also, explain the range of opinions on the subject.

4. **Evaluation:** Write a paragraph that evaluates Jacobowitz's essay.

Getting Ready to Write: Form, Process, and Purpose

Four elements are key to good writing. Keep them in mind whenever you write.

Four Basics of Good Writing

1 It considers what the audience knows and needs.

2 It fulfills the writer's purpose.

3 It includes a clear, definite point.

4 It provides support that shows, explains, or proves the main point.

This chapter discusses the four basics in more detail. It also outlines the writing process and shows you how to get started by choosing something to write about.

NOTE: AVOIDING PLAGIARISM

In all the writing you do, it is important to avoid plagiarism—using other people's words or information as your own. Your instructors are aware of plagiarism and know how to look for it. Writers who plagiarize, either on purpose or by accident, risk failing a course or losing their jobs and damaging their reputations.

To avoid accidental plagiarism, take careful notes on every source (books, interviews, television shows, Web sites, and so on) you might use in your writing. When recording information from sources, take notes in your own words, unless you plan to use direct quotations. In that case, make sure to record the quotation word for word. Also, include quotation marks around it, both in your notes and in your paper.

TIP For more on avoiding plagiarism and citing and documenting outside sources, visit the Bedford/ St. Martin's Workshop on Plagiarism at http://bcs .bedfordstmartins .com/plagiarism.

LearningCurve For extra practice in the skills covered in this chapter, visit: bedfordstmartins.com/rwinteractive.

When you use material from other sources—whether you directly quote or put information in your own words (paraphrase)—you must name and give citation information about these sources.

Paragraph and Essay Form

In this course (and in the rest of college), you will write paragraphs and essays. Each kind of writing has a basic structure.

PARAGRAPH FORM

A **paragraph** has three necessary parts: the topic sentence, the body, and the concluding sentence.

PARAGRAPH PART	PURPOSE OF THE PARAGRAPH PART
1. The **topic sentence**	states the **main point**. The topic sentence is often the first sentence of the paragraph.
2. The **body**	supports (shows, explains, or proves) the main point with **support sentences** that contain facts and details.
3. The **concluding sentence**	reminds readers of the main point and often makes an observation.

ESSAY FORM

An **essay** is a piece of writing that examines a topic in more depth than a paragraph. A short essay may have four or five paragraphs, totaling three hundred to six hundred words. A long essay may be many pages long, depending on what the essay needs to accomplish, such as persuading someone to do something, using research to make a point, or explaining a complex concept.

An essay has three necessary parts: the introduction, the body, and the conclusion.

ESSAY PART	PURPOSE OF THE ESSAY PART
1. The **introduction**	states the **main point**, or **thesis**, generally in a single, strong statement. The introduction may be a single paragraph or multiple paragraphs.

ESSAY PART	PURPOSE OF THE ESSAY PART
2. The **body**	supports (shows, explains, or proves) the main point. It generally has at least three **support paragraphs**, each containing facts and details that develop the main point. Each support paragraph has a **topic sentence** that supports the thesis statement.
3. The **conclusion**	reminds readers of the main point and makes an observation. Often, it also summarizes and reinforces the support.

The following diagram shows how the parts of an essay correspond to the parts of a paragraph.

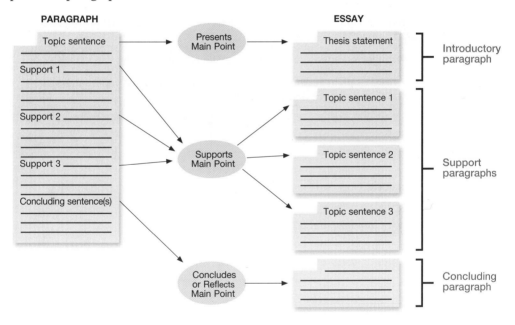

The Writing Process

The chart that follows shows the four stages of the **writing process**, all steps you will follow to write well, whether you are writing a paragraph or an essay. Keep in mind that you may not always go in a straight line through the four stages; instead, you might circle back to earlier steps to further improve your writing.

THE WRITING PROCESS

Generate ideas

CONSIDER: What is my purpose in writing? Given this purpose, what interests me? Who will read this paper? What do they need to know?

- Determine your audience and purpose (pages 21–22).
- Find and explore your topic (pages 23–28).
- Make your point (pages 29–37).
- Support your point (pages 37–41).

Draft

CONSIDER: How can I organize my ideas effectively and show my readers what I mean?

- Arrange your ideas, and make an outline (pages 42–45).
- Write a draft, including an introduction that will interest your readers, a strong conclusion, and a title (pages 46–51).

Revise

CONSIDER: How can I make my draft clearer or more convincing to my readers?

- Look for ideas that do not fit (pages 54–55).
- Look for ideas that could use more detailed support (pages 55–56).
- Connect ideas with transitional words and sentences (pages 56–57).

Edit

CONSIDER: What errors could confuse my readers and weaken my point?

- Find and correct the most serious errors in grammar (Chapter 15).
- Look for other errors in style and grammar (Chapter 16).
- Check your punctuation and capitalization (Chapter 17).

Audience and Purpose

Your **audience** is the person or people who will read what you write. In college, your audience is usually your instructors. Whenever you write, always have at least one real person in mind as a reader. Think about what that person already knows and what he or she will need to know to understand your main point.

Your **purpose** is your reason for writing. Let's take a look at some different audiences and purposes.

Audience and Purpose

TYPE OF WRITING	AUDIENCE AND PURPOSE	TIPS
COLLEGE: A research essay about the environmental effects of "fracking": fracturing rock layers to extract oil or natural gas	**AUDIENCE:** The professor of your environmental science class **PURPOSE:** • To complete an assignment according to instructions • To show what you have learned about the topic	When writing to fulfill an assignment, never assume "My instructor already knows this fact, so what's the point of mentioning it?" By providing relevant examples and details, you demonstrate your knowledge of a subject.
WORK: An e-mail to coworkers about your company's new insurance provider	**AUDIENCE:** Fellow workers **PURPOSE:** To make sure that coworkers understand all the important details about the new provider	Define or explain any terminology or concepts that will not be familiar to your audience.
EVERYDAY LIFE: An electronic comment about an online newspaper editorial that you disagree with	**AUDIENCE:** • The editorial writer • Other readers of the editorial **PURPOSE:** To make the editorial writer and other readers aware of your views	Keep all correspondence with others as polite as possible, even if you disagree with their views.

The tone and content of your writing will vary depending on your audiences and purposes. In some cases, such as text messages or e-mails with friends, it makes sense to use informal English. However, in college, at work, and in your everyday life, when you are speaking or writing to someone in authority for a serious purpose, use formal English; people will take you seriously.

PRACTICE 1   Writing for a Formal Audience

A student, Terri Travers, sent the following text message to a friend to complain about not getting into a criminal justice course. Rewrite the text as if you were Terri and you were writing an e-mail to Professor Wexner. The purpose is to ask whether the professor would consider allowing you into the class given that you signed up early and have the necessary grades.

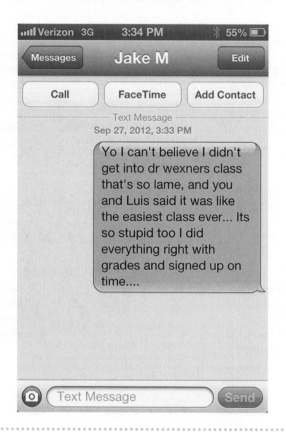

Finding, Narrowing, and Exploring Your Topic

A **topic** is who or what you are writing about. It is the subject of your paragraph or essay.

QUESTIONS FOR FINDING A GOOD TOPIC

- Does this topic interest me? If so, why do I care about it?
- Do I know something about the topic? Do I want to know more?
- Can I get involved with some part of the topic? Is it relevant to my life in some way?
- Is the topic specific enough for the assignment (a paragraph or a short essay)?

Choose one of the following topics or one of your own and focus on one part of it that you are familiar with. (For example, focus on one personal goal or a specific problem of working students that interests you.)

Music/group I like	Sports
Problems of working students	An essential survival skill
An activity/group I am involved in	A personal goal

Use the general topic you have chosen to complete the practice exercises on pages 25 and 28.

Narrowing a Topic

If your instructor assigns a general topic, it may at first seem uninteresting, unfamiliar, or too general. It is up to you to find a good, specific topic based on the general one. Whether the topic is your own or assigned, you next need to narrow and explore it. To **narrow** a general topic, focus on the smaller parts of it until you find one that is interesting and specific.

Here are some ways to narrow a general topic.

DIVIDE IT INTO SMALLER CATEGORIES

GENERAL TOPIC **A personal goal**

Lose weight

Get a degree

Make more money

THINK OF SPECIFIC EXAMPLES FROM YOUR LIFE

GENERAL TOPIC **Social media**

Twitter (which feeds do I follow regularly? what do I get from them?)

Facebook (what features are fun or useful? what feels like a waste of time?)

Google+ (is it just another Facebook, or is it truly different?)

THINK OF SPECIFIC EXAMPLES FROM CURRENT EVENTS

GENERAL TOPIC **Heroism**

The guy who pulled a stranger from a burning car

The people who stopped a robbery downtown

QUESTION YOUR ASSUMPTIONS

Questioning assumptions—an important part of critical thinking (see Chapter 1)—can be a good way to narrow a topic. First, identify any assumptions you have about your topic. Then, question them, playing "devil's advocate"; in other words, imagine what someone with a different point of view might say.

GENERAL TOPIC: Video Games

POSSIBLE ASSUMPTIONS	QUESTIONS
Video game pros:	
• Kids get rewarded with good scores for staying focused. →	Does staying focused on a video game mean that a kid will stay focused on homework or in class?
• Video games can teach some useful skills. →	Like what? How am I defining "useful"?
Video game cons:	
• They make kids more violent. →	Is there really any proof for that? What do experts say?
• They have no real educational value. →	Didn't my niece say that some video game helped her learn to read?

Next, ask yourself what assumptions and questions interest you the most. Then, focus on those interests.

When you have found a promising topic for a paragraph or essay, be sure to test it by using the Questions for Finding a Good Topic on page 23. You may need to narrow and test your ideas several times before you find a topic that will work for the assignment.

A topic for an essay can be a little broader than one for a paragraph because essays are longer than paragraphs and allow you to develop more ideas. But be careful: Most of the extra length in an essay should come from developing ideas in more depth (giving more examples and details, explaining what you mean), not from covering a broader topic.

Read the following examples of how a general topic was narrowed to a more specific topic for an essay and an even more specific topic for a paragraph.

GENERAL TOPIC		NARROWED ESSAY TOPIC		NARROWED PARAGRAPH TOPIC
Internships	→	How internships can help you get a job	→	One or two important things you can learn from an internship
Public service opportunities	→	Volunteering at a homeless shelter	→	My first impression of the homeless shelter

PRACTICE 2   Narrowing a General Topic

Use one of the four methods above to narrow your topic. Then, ask yourself the Questions for Finding a Good Topic (from page 23).

Exploring Your Topic

Prewriting techniques can give you ideas at any time during your writing: to find a topic, to get ideas for what you want to say about it, and to support your ideas. Ask yourself: What interests me about this topic? What do I know? What do I want to say? Then, use one or more of the prewriting techniques to find the answers.

PREWRITING TECHNIQUES

- Freewriting
- Listing/brainstorming
- Discussing
- Clustering/mapping
- Using the Internet
- Keeping a journal

When prewriting, your goal is to come up with as many ideas as possible. Do not say, "Oh, that's stupid" or "That won't work." Just get your brain working by writing down all the possibilities.

FREEWRITING

Freewriting is like having a conversation with yourself, on paper. To free-write, just start writing everything you can think of about your topic. Write nonstop for five minutes. Do not go back and cross anything out, and do not worry about using correct grammar or spelling; just write. Here is a student's freewriting on the topic of getting a college degree:

> So I know I want to get a college degree even though sometimes I wonder if I ever can make it because it's so hard with work and my two-year-old daughter and no money and a car that needs work. I can't take more than two courses at a time and even then I hardly get a chance to sleep if I want to do any of the assignments or study. But I have to think I'll get a better job because this one at the restaurant is driving me nuts and doesn't pay much so I have to work a lot with a boss I can't stand and still wonder how I'm gonna pay the bills. I know life can be better if I can just manage to become a nurse. I'll make more money and can live anywhere I want because everyplace needs nurses. I won't have to work at a job where I am not respected by anyone. I want respect, I know I'm hardworking and smart and good with people and deserve better than this. So does my daughter. No one in my family has ever graduated from college even though my sister took two courses, but then she stopped. I know I can do this, I just have to make a commitment to do it and not look away.

LISTING / BRAINSTORMING

List all the ideas about your topic that you can think of. Write as many as you can in five minutes without stopping.

> <u>GETTING A COLLEGE DEGREE</u>
>
> want a better life for myself and my daughter
>
> want to be a nurse and help care for people
>
> make more money
>
> not have to work so many hours
>
> could live where I want in a nicer place
>
> good future and benefits like health insurance
>
> get respect
>
> proud of myself, achieve, show everyone
>
> be a professional, work in a clean place

Discussing

Many people find it helpful to discuss ideas with another person before they write. As they talk, they get more ideas and immediate feedback.

If you and your discussion partner both have writing assignments, first explore one person's topic and then explore the other's. The person whose topic is being explored is the interviewee; the other person is the interviewer. The interviewer should ask questions about anything that seems unclear and should let the interviewee know what sounds interesting. In addition, the interviewer should identify and try to question any assumptions the interviewee seems to be making (see page 24). The interviewee should give thoughtful answers and keep an open mind. He or she should also take notes.

Clustering / Mapping

Clustering, also called mapping, is like listing except that you arrange your ideas visually. Start by writing your narrowed topic in the center. Then, write the questions Why? What interests me? and What do I want to say? around the narrowed topic. Write at least three answers to each question. Keep branching out from the ideas until you feel you have fully explored your topic.

Using the Internet

Go to **www.google.com**, and type in specific key words about your topic. The search will provide more results than you can use, but it will help you with ideas for your paper. Make notes about important or useful ideas you get from the Internet.

Keeping a Journal

Setting aside a few minutes on a regular schedule to write in a journal will give you a great source of ideas when you need them. What you write does not need to be long or formal. You can use a journal in several ways:

- To record and explore your personal thoughts and feelings
- To comment on things that happen, to you personally or in politics, in your neighborhood, at work, in college, and so on
- To explore situations you do not understand (as you write, you may figure them out)

....

PRACTICE 3 Exploring Your Narrowed Topic

Use two or three prewriting techniques to explore your narrowed topic.

....

WRITING ASSIGNMENT

Review your narrowed topic (recorded in Practice 2) and ideas from your prewriting. Use the checklist that follows to make sure your topic and ideas about it are clear. If necessary, spend some more time clarifying your topic or generating ideas before moving on to Chapter 3.

CHECKLIST

Evaluating Your Narrowed Topic

- ☐ This topic interests me.
- ☐ My narrowed topic is specific.
- ☐ I can write about it in a paragraph or an essay (whichever you have been assigned).
- ☐ I have generated some things to say about this topic.

3

Organizing Your Main Point and Support

Arranging Your Ideas

Once you have settled on a topic to write about (see Chapter 2), you need to determine what your main point will be and how you will support that point.

Topic Sentences and Thesis Statements

Every good piece of writing has a **main point**—what the writer wants to get across to the readers about the topic or the writer's position on that topic. A **topic sentence** (for a paragraph) and a **thesis statement** (for an essay) express the writer's main point. To see the relationship between the thesis statement of an essay and the topic sentences of paragraphs that support a thesis statement, see the diagram on page 19.

In many paragraphs, the main point is expressed in either the first or last sentence. In essays, the thesis statement is usually one sentence (often the first or last) in an introductory paragraph that contains several other sentences related to the main point.

One way to write a topic sentence for a paragraph or a thesis statement for an essay is to use this basic formula as a start:

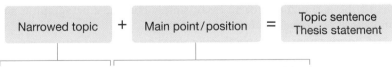

| Narrowed topic | + | Main point/position | = | Topic sentence
Thesis statement |

The tutoring center has helped me improve my writing.

A good topic sentence or thesis statement has several basic features.

BASICS OF A GOOD TOPIC SENTENCE OR THESIS STATEMENT

- It fits the size of the assignment.
- It states a single main point or position about a topic.
- It is specific.
- It is something you can show, explain, or prove.
- It is forceful.

The explanations and practices in the following five sections, organized according to the "basics" described above, will help you write good topic sentences and thesis statements.

Fitting the Size of the Assignment

As you develop a topic sentence or thesis statement, think carefully about the length of the assignment.

Sometimes, a main-point statement can be the same for a paragraph or essay.

> Although they are entering the job market in tough economic times, Millennials have some important advantages in the workplace.
>
>   Topic   Main point

If the writer had been assigned a paragraph, she might follow the main point with support sentences and a concluding sentence like those in the "paragraph" diagram on page 19.

If the writer had been assigned an essay, she might develop the same support, but instead of writing single sentences to support her main idea, she would develop each support point into a paragraph. The support sentences she wrote in a paragraph might be topic sentences for support paragraphs. (For more on providing support, see pages 37–41.)

Often, however, a topic sentence for a paragraph is much narrower than a thesis statement for an essay, simply because a paragraph is shorter and allows less development of ideas.

Consider how one general topic could be narrowed into an essay topic and into an even more specific paragraph topic.

GENERAL TOPIC	NARROWED ESSAY TOPIC	NARROWED PARAGRAPH TOPIC
Internships →	How internships can help you get a job →	One or two important things you can learn from an internship

POSSIBLE THESIS STATEMENT (ESSAY)	The skills and connections you gain through a summer internship can help you get a good job after graduation.
POSSIBLE TOPIC SENTENCE (PARAGRAPH)	A summer internship is a good way to test whether a particular career is right for you.

PRACTICE 1 Writing Sentences to Fit the Assignment

For each of the topics below, write a thesis statement for the narrowed essay topic and a topic sentence for the narrowed paragraph topic.

EXAMPLE:

GENERAL TOPIC: Sports

NARROWED FOR AN ESSAY: Competition in school sports

POSSIBLE THESIS STATEMENT: *Competition in school sports has reached dangerous levels.*

NARROWED FOR A PARAGRAPH: User fees for school sports

POSSIBLE TOPIC SENTENCE: *This year's user fees for participation in school sports are too high.*

1. GENERAL TOPIC: Public service opportunities

NARROWED FOR AN ESSAY: Volunteering at a homeless shelter

NARROWED FOR A PARAGRAPH: My first impression of the homeless shelter

2.   **GENERAL TOPIC:** A personal goal

NARROWED FOR AN ESSAY: Getting healthy

NARROWED FOR A PARAGRAPH: Eating the right foods

3.   **GENERAL TOPIC:** A great vacation

NARROWED FOR AN ESSAY: A family camping trip

NARROWED FOR A PARAGRAPH: A lesson I learned on our family camping trip

Some topic sentences or thesis statements are too broad for either a short essay or a paragraph. A main idea that is too broad is impossible to show, explain, or prove within the space of a paragraph or short essay.

TOO BROAD   Art is important.

[How could a writer possibly support such a broad concept in a paragraph or essay?]

NARROWER   Art instruction for young children has surprising benefits.

A topic sentence or thesis statement that is too narrow leaves the writer with little to write about. There is little to show, explain, or prove.

TOO NARROW   Buy rechargeable batteries.

[OK, so now what?]

BROADER   Choosing rechargeable batteries over conventional batteries is one action you can take to reduce your effect on the environment.

PRACTICE 2   Writing Topic Sentences That Are Neither Too Broad Nor Too Narrow

In the following five practice items, three of the topic sentences are either too broad or too narrow, and two of them are OK. Rewrite the three weak sentences to make them broader or narrower as needed.

EXAMPLE: Life can be tough for soldiers when they come home.

NARROWER: *We are not providing our returning soldiers with enough help in readjusting to civilian life.*

1.   I take public transportation to work.

2.   Because of state and national education budget cuts, schools are having to lay off teachers and cut important programs.

3.   College is challenging.

4.   I would like to be successful in life.

5.   Having a positive attitude improves people's ability to function, improves their interactions with others, and reduces stress.

Focusing on a Single Main Point

Your topic sentence or thesis statement should focus on only one main point. Two main points can split and weaken the focus of the writing.

MAIN IDEA WITH TWO MAIN POINTS

High schools should sell healthy food instead of junk food, and they should start later in the morning.

The two main points are underlined. Although both are good main points, together they split both the writer's and the readers' focus. The writer would need to give reasons to support each point, and the ideas are completely different.

MAIN IDEA WITH A SINGLE MAIN POINT

High schools should sell healthy food instead of junk food.

OR

High schools should start later in the morning.

PRACTICE 3   Writing Sentences with a Single Main Point

Determine which of the following sentences, have more than one main point.

> **EXAMPLE:**   Shopping at secondhand stores is a fun way to save money, and you can meet all kinds of interesting people as you shop. *Two main points underlined.*

1. My younger sister, the baby of the family, was the most adventurous of my four siblings.
2. Servicing hybrid cars is a growing part of automotive technology education, and dealers cannot keep enough hybrids in stock.
3. My brother, Bobby, is incredibly creative, and he takes in stray animals.
4. Pets can actually bring families together, and they require lots of care.
5. Unless people conserve voluntarily, we will deplete our water supply.

Being Specific

A good topic sentence or thesis statement gives readers specific information so that they know exactly what the writer's main point is.

GENERAL   Students are often overwhelmed.

[How are students overwhelmed?]

SPECIFIC   Working college students have to learn how to juggle many responsibilities.

One way to make sure your topic sentence or thesis statement is specific is to make it a preview of what you are planning to say in the rest of the paragraph or essay. Just be certain that every point you preview is closely related to your main idea.

PREVIEW: Working college students have to learn how to juggle many responsibilities: doing a good job at work, getting to class regularly and on time, being alert in class, and doing the homework assignments.

PREVIEW: I have a set routine every Saturday morning that includes sleeping late, going to the gym, and shopping for food.

PRACTICE 4   Writing Sentences That Are Specific

Revise each of the sentences below to make it more specific. There is no one correct answer. As you read the sentences, think about what would make them more understandable to you if you were about to read a paragraph or essay on the topic.

EXAMPLE: Marriage can be a wonderful thing.

Marriage to the right person can add love, companionship, and support to life.

1.   My job is horrible.

2.   Working with others is rewarding.

3.   I am a good worker.

4.   This place could use a lot of improvement.

5.   Getting my driver's license was challenging.

Using an Idea You Can Show, Explain, or Prove

If a main point is so obvious that it does not need support or if it states a simple fact, you will not have much to say about it.

OBVIOUS	Many people like to take vacations in the summer.
REVISED	The vast and incredible beauty of the Grand Canyon draws crowds of visitors each summer.
FACT	Three hundred cities worldwide have bicycle-sharing programs.
REVISED	Bicycle-sharing programs are popular, but funding them long-term can be challenging for cities with tight budgets.

PRACTICE 5   Writing Sentences with Ideas You Can Show, Explain, or Prove

Revise the following sentences so that they contain an idea you could show, explain, or prove.

EXAMPLE: Leasing a car is popular.

Leasing a car has many advantages over buying one.

1.   Texting while driving is dangerous.

2.   My monthly rent is $750.

3.   Health insurance rates rise every year.

4.   Many people in this country work for minimum wage.

5.   Technology is becoming increasingly important.

Being Forceful

A good topic sentence or thesis statement is forceful. Do not say you *will* make a point; just make it. Do not say "I think." Just state your point.

WEAK	In my opinion, everyone should exercise.
FORCEFUL	Everyone should exercise to reduce stress, maintain a healthy weight, and feel better overall.
WEAK	I think student fees are much too high.
FORCEFUL	Student fees need to be explained and justified.

PRACTICE 6   Writing Forceful Sentences

Rewrite the following sentences to make them more forceful. Also, add details to make the sentences more specific.

> **EXAMPLE:** Jason's Market is the best.
>
> *Jason's Market is clean, organized, and filled with quality products.*

1. I will prove that drug testing in the workplace is an invasion of privacy.
2. This school does not allow cell phones in class.
3. I strongly think I deserve a raise.
4. Nancy should be the head of the Students' Association.
5. I think my neighborhood is nice.

WRITING ASSIGNMENT

Write a topic sentence or thesis statement using the narrowed topic you developed in Chapter 2 or one of the following topics (which you will have to narrow).

Community service	Holiday traditions
A controversial issue	A strong belief
Dressing for success	Snitching

After writing your topic sentence or thesis statement, complete the checklist that follows.

CHECKLIST

Evaluating Your Main Point

- ☐ It is a complete sentence.
- ☐ It includes my topic and the main point I want to make about it.
- ☐ It fits the assignment.
- ☐ It states a single main point.
- ☐ It is specific.
- ☐ It is something I can show, explain, or prove.
- ☐ It is forceful.

Support for Your Main Point

Support is the collection of examples, facts, or evidence that shows, explains, or proves your main point. **Primary support points** are the major ideas that back up your main point, and **secondary support** gives details to back up your primary support.

Key Features of Good Support

Without support, you *state* the main point, but you do not *make* the main point. Consider these unsupported statements:

> The amount shown on my bill is incorrect.
> I deserve a raise.
> I am innocent of the crime.

The statements may be true, but without good support, they are not convincing. If you sometimes get papers back with the comment "You need to support/develop your ideas," the suggestions in this chapter will help you.

Also, keep in mind that the same point repeated several times is not support. It is just repetition.

REPETITION, NOT SUPPORT   The amount shown on my bill is incorrect. You overcharged me. It didn't cost that much. The total is wrong.

SUPPORT   The amount shown on my bill is incorrect. I ordered the bacon-cheeseburger plate, which is $6.99 on the menu. On the bill, the order is correct, but the amount is $16.99.

As you develop support for your main point, make sure it has these three features.

BASICS OF GOOD SUPPORT

- It relates directly to your main point. Remember that the purpose of support is to show, explain, or prove your main point.

- It considers your readers and what they will need to know.

- It gives readers enough specific details, particularly through examples, so that they can see what you mean.

Support in Paragraphs versus Essays

In paragraphs, your main point is expressed in a topic sentence. In both paragraphs and essays, it is important to add enough details (secondary support) about the primary support to make the main point clear to readers.

In the following paragraph, the topic sentence is underlined twice, the primary support is underlined once, and the details for each primary support point are in italics.

When I first enrolled in college, I thought that studying history was a waste of time. But after taking two world history classes, I have come to the conclusion that these courses count for far more than some credit hours in my college record. First, learning about historical events has helped me put important current events in perspective. *For instance, by studying the history of migration around the world, I have learned that immigration has been going on for hundreds of years. In addition, it is common in many countries, not just the United States. I have also learned about ways in which various societies have debated immigration, just as Americans are doing today.* Second, history courses have taught me about the power that individual people can have, even under very challenging circumstances. *I was especially inspired by the story of Toussaint L'Ouverture, a former slave who, in the 1790s, led uprisings in the French colony of Saint-Domingue, transforming it into the independent nation of Haiti. Although L'Ouverture faced difficult odds, he persisted and achieved great things.* The biggest benefit of taking history courses is that they have encouraged me to dig more deeply into subjects than I ever have before. *For a paper about the lasting influence of Anne Frank,[1] I drew on quotations from her famous diary, on biographies about her, and on essays written by noted historians. The research was fascinating, and I loved piecing together the various facts and insights to come to my own conclusions.* To sum up, I have become hooked on history, and I have a feeling that the lessons it teaches me will be relevant far beyond college.

[1] **Anne Frank (1929–1945):** a German Jewish girl who fled to the Netherlands with her family after Adolf Hitler, leader of the Nazi Party, became chancellor of Germany. In 1944, Anne and her family were arrested by the Nazis, and she died in a concentration camp the following year.

In an essay, each primary support point, along with its supporting details, is developed into a separate paragraph. (See the diagram on page 19.) Specifically, each underlined point in the previous paragraph could be turned into a topic sentence that would be supported by the italicized details. However, in preparing an essay on the preceding topic, the writer would want to add more details and examples for each primary support point.

Generating Support

To generate support for the main point of a paragraph or essay, try one or more of the following strategies.

THREE QUICK STRATEGIES FOR GENERATING SUPPORT

1. *Circle an important word or phrase* in your topic sentence (for a paragraph) or thesis statement (for an essay), and write about it for a few minutes. As you work, refer back to your main point to make sure you're on the right track.

2. *Reread your topic sentence or thesis statement, and write down the first thought you have.* Then, write down your next thought. Keep going.

3. *Use a prewriting technique* (freewriting, listing, discussing, clustering, and so on) while thinking about your main point and your audience. Write for three to five minutes without stopping.

PRACTICE 7   Generating Supporting Ideas

Choose one of the following sentences, or your own topic sentence or thesis statement, and use one of the three strategies on p. 39 to generate at least twelve supporting points. Keep your answers for use in later practices in this chapter.

1. Some television shows stir my mind instead of numbing it.

2. Today there is no such thing as a "typical" college student.

3. Learning happens not only in school but throughout a person's life.

4. Practical intelligence can't be measured by grades.

5. I deserve a raise.

Selecting the Best Primary Support

After you have generated possible support, review your ideas; then, select the best ones to use as primary support. Here you take control of your topic, shaping the way readers will see it and the main point you are making about it. The following steps can help.

1. Carefully read the ideas you have generated.

2. Select three to five primary support points that will be clearest and most convincing to your readers, providing the best examples, facts, and observations to support your main point. If you are writing a paragraph, these points will become the primary support for your topic sentence. If you are writing an essay, they will become topic sentences of the individual paragraphs that support your thesis statement.

3. Cross out ideas that are not closely related to your main point.

4. If you find that you have crossed out most of your ideas and do not have enough left to support your main point, use one of the three strategies from page 39 to find more.

PRACTICE 8   Selecting the Best Support

Refer to your response to Practice 7 (above). Of your possible primary support points, choose three to five that you think will best show, explain, or prove your main point to your readers.

Adding Secondary Support

Once you have selected your best primary support points, you need to flesh them out for your readers. Do this by adding **secondary support**, specific examples, facts, and observations to back up your primary support points.

· ·

PRACTICE 9   Adding Secondary Support

Using your answers to Practice 8, choose three primary support points, and write them down. Then, read each of them carefully, and write down at least three supporting details (secondary support) for each one. For examples of secondary support, see the example paragraph on pages 38–39.

· ·

WRITING ASSIGNMENT

Develop primary support points and supporting details using the topic sentence or thesis statement you developed at the beginning of this chapter or one of the following topic sentences/thesis statements.

Same-sex marriages should/should not be legal in all fifty states.

The drinking age should/should not be lowered.

All families have some unique family traditions.

People who do not speak "proper" English are discriminated against.

Many movies have important messages for viewers.

· ·

After developing your support, complete the following checklist.

CHECKLIST

Evaluating Your Support

☐ It is directly related to my main point.

☐ It uses examples, facts, and observations that will make sense to my readers.

☐ It includes enough specific details to show my readers exactly what I mean.

Once you have pulled together your primary support points and secondary supporting details, you are ready to put your ideas in order.

Arrange Your Ideas

In writing, **order** means the sequence in which you present your ideas: What comes first, what comes next, and so on. There are three common ways of ordering—arranging—your ideas: **time order** (also called chronological order), **space order**, and **order of importance**.

Read the paragraph examples that follow. In each paragraph, the topic sentences are underlined twice, the primary support points are underlined once, and the secondary support is in italics.

Use Time Order to Write about Events

Use **time order** (chronological order) to arrange points according to when they happened. Time order works best when you are writing about events.

EXAMPLE USING TIME ORDER

Officer Meredith Pavlovic's traffic stop of August 23, 2011, was fairly typical of an investigation and arrest for drunk driving. First, at around 12:15 a.m. that day, she noticed that the driver of a blue Honda Civic was acting suspiciously. *The car was weaving between the fast and center lanes of Interstate 93 North near exit 12. In addition, it was proceeding at approximately 45 mph in a 55 mph zone.* Therefore, Officer Pavlovic took the second step of pulling the driver over for a closer investigation. *The driver's license told Officer Pavlovic that the driver was twenty-six-year-old Paul Brownwell. Brownwell's red eyes, slurred speech, and alcohol-tainted breath told Officer Pavlovic that Brownwell was very drunk.* But she had to be absolutely sure. Thus, as a next step, she tested his balance and blood alcohol level. *The results were that Brownwell could barely get out of the car, let alone stand on one foot. Also, a breathalyzer test showed that his blood alcohol level was 0.13, well over the legal limit of 0.08.* These results meant an arrest for Brownwell, an unfortunate outcome for him, but a lucky one for other people on the road at that time.

Use Space Order to Describe Objects, Places, or People

Use **space order** to arrange ideas so that your readers picture your topic the way you see it. Space order usually works best when you are writing about a physical object or place, or a person's appearance.

EXAMPLE USING SPACE ORDER

Donna looked professional for her interview. Her long, dark, curly hair was held back with a gold clip. *No stray wisps escaped. Normally wild and unruly, her hair was smooth, shiny, and neat.* She wore a white silk blouse *with just the top button open at her throat. Donna had made sure to leave time to iron it so that it wouldn't be wrinkled. The blouse was neatly tucked into her* black A-line skirt, *which came just to the top of her knee.* She wore black stockings *that she had checked for runs and* black low-heeled shoes. Altogether, her appearance marked her as serious and professional, and she was sure to make a good first impression.

Use Order of Importance to Emphasize a Particular Point

Use **order of importance** to arrange points according to their significance, interest, or surprise value. Usually, save the most important point for last.

EXAMPLE USING ORDER OF IMPORTANCE

People who keep guns in their homes risk endangering both themselves and others. Many accidental injuries occur when a weapon is improperly stored or handled. *For example, someone cleaning a closet where a loaded gun is stored may handle the gun in a way that causes it to go off and injure him or her.* Guns also feature in many reports of "crimes of passion." *A couple with a violent history has a fight, and, in a fit of rage, one gets the gun and shoots the other, wounding or killing the other person.* Most common and most tragic are incidents in which children find loaded guns and play with them, accidentally killing themselves or their playmates. Considering these factors, the risks of keeping guns in the home outweigh the advantages, for many people.

Planning Your Draft

When you have decided how to order your primary support points, it is time to make a more detailed plan for your paragraph or essay. A good, visual way to plan a draft is to arrange your ideas in an outline. An **outline** lists the topic sentence (for a paragraph) or thesis statement (for an essay), the primary support points for the topic sentence or thesis statement, and secondary supporting details for each of the support points. It provides a map of your ideas that you can follow as you write.

The examples below are in "formal" outline form, with letters and numbers to distinguish between primary supporting and secondary supporting details. Some instructors require this format. If you are making an outline just for yourself, you might choose to write a less formal outline, simply indenting the secondary supporting details under the primary support rather than using numbers and letters.

SAMPLE OUTLINE FOR A PARAGRAPH

Topic sentence
    A.   **Primary support sentence 1**
        1.   Supporting detail sentence 1
        2.   Supporting detail sentence 2 (optional)
    B.   **Primary support sentence 2**
        1.   Supporting detail sentence 1
        2.   Supporting detail sentence 2 (optional)
    C.   **Primary support sentence 3**
        1.   Supporting detail sentence 1
        2.   Supporting detail sentence 2 (optional)

Concluding sentence

SAMPLE OUTLINE FOR A FIVE-PARAGRAPH ESSAY

Thesis statement (part of introductory paragraph 1)
    A.   **Topic sentence for support point 1** (paragraph 2)
        1.   Supporting detail 1 for support point 1
        2.   Supporting detail 2 for support point 1 (and so on)
    B.   **Topic sentence for support point 2** (paragraph 3)
        1.   Supporting detail 1 for support point 2
        2.   Supporting detail 2 for support point 2 (and so on)
    C.   **Topic sentence for support point 3** (paragraph 4)
        1.   Supporting detail 1 for support point 3
        2.   Supporting detail 2 for support point 3 (and so on)

Concluding paragraph (paragraph 5)

· ·

PRACTICE 10   Making an Outline

Reread the paragraph on page 42 that illustrates time order of organization. Then, make an outline for it.

· ·

WRITING ASSIGNMENT

Create an outline using your topic sentence or thesis statement along with the primary support points and supporting details you have developed in this chapter. Arrange your ideas according to time order, space order, or order of importance.

· ·

After creating your outline, complete the following checklist.

CHECKLIST

Evaluating Your Outline

- ☐ It includes my topic sentence or thesis statement.
- ☐ It includes at least three supporting points.
- ☐ Each supporting point has at least one supporting detail.
- ☐ It is organized according to time order, space order, or order of importance.
- ☐ If required by my instructor, it is prepared in formal outline format.

You now have a clear main point with support, organized in a logical way. In the next chapter you will begin drafting your paragraph or essay.

4

Drafting and Revising Paragraphs and Essays

Putting Your Ideas Together

A **draft** is the first whole version of all your ideas put together in a piece of writing. Do the best job you can in drafting, but know that you can make changes later.

BASICS OF A GOOD DRAFT

- It has a topic sentence (for a paragraph) and a thesis statement (for an essay) that makes a clear main point.

- It has a logical organization of ideas.

- It has primary and secondary support that shows, explains, or proves the main point.

- It has a conclusion that makes an observation about the main point.

- It follows standard paragraph form (see page 18) or standard essay form (see pages 18–19).

Drafting Paragraphs

Use Complete Sentences

Write your draft with your outline in front of you. Be sure to include your topic sentence, and express each point in a complete sentence. As you write, you may want to add support or change the order. It is OK to make changes from your outline as you write.

✓ LearningCurve For extra practice in the skills covered in this chapter, visit: bedfordstmartins.com/rwinteractive.

Consider Introductory Techniques

Although paragraphs typically begin with topic sentences, they may also begin with a quote, an example, or a surprising fact or idea. The topic sentence is then presented later in the paragraph. For examples of various introductory techniques, see pages 49–50. For more on topic sentences, see pages 29–37.

End with a Concluding Sentence

A **concluding sentence** refers back to the main point and makes an observation based on what you have written. The concluding sentence does not just repeat the topic sentence. Concluding paragraphs for essays are discussed on pages 50–51.

Title Your Paragraph

The title is the first thing readers see, so it should give them a good idea of what your paragraph is about. Decide on a title by rereading your draft, especially your topic sentence. A paragraph title should not repeat your topic sentence. Titles for essays are discussed on page 51.

    NOTE: Center your title at the top of the page before the first paragraph. Do not put quotation marks around it or underline it.

Drafting Essays

The draft of an essay has all the basics listed on pages 46–47. In addition,

- The essay should include an introductory paragraph that draws readers in and includes the thesis statement.
- The topic sentences for the paragraphs that follow the introduction should directly support the thesis statement. In turn, each topic sentence should be backed by enough support.
- The conclusion should be a full paragraph rather than a single sentence.

Sample Student Paragraph

Identifying
information

Title indicates
main point

Topic sentence
(indented first
line)

Support
point 1

Supporting
details

Support
point 2

Supporting
details

Support
point 3

Supporting
details

Concluding
sentence
(refers back
to main point)

Chelsea Wilson
Professor Holmes
EN 099
September 7, 2012

My Career Goal

    My career goal is to become a nurse because it offers so much that I value. Being a nurse is a good and practical job. Licensed practical nurses make an average of $40,000 per year. That amount is much more than I make now working long hours at a minimum-wage job in a restaurant. Working as a nurse, I could be a better provider for my daughter. I could also spend more time with her. Also, nursing is more than just a job; it is a profession. As a nurse, I will help people who are sick, and helping people is important to me. With time, I will be able to grow within the profession, like becoming a registered nurse who makes more money and has more responsibility. Because nursing is a profession, nurses are respected. When I become a nurse, I will respect myself and be proud of myself for reaching my goal, even though I know it will take a lot of hard work. The most important thing about becoming a nurse is that it will be good for my young daughter. I will be a good role model for her. For all of these reasons, my goal is to become a nurse. Reaching this goal is important to me and worth the work.

• •

WRITING ASSIGNMENT   **Paragraph**

Write a draft paragraph, using the material you have developed up to this point or working with one of the following topic sentences. If you use one of the topic sentences below, you may want to revise it to fit what you want to say.

Being a good _____ requires _____.

I can find any number of ways to waste my time.

People tell me I am _____, and I guess I have to agree.

So many decisions are involved in going to college.

The most important thing to me in life is _____.

• •

After writing your draft paragraph, complete the following checklist.

CHECKLIST

Evaluating Your Draft Paragraph

- ☐ It has a clear, confident topic sentence that states my main point.
- ☐ Each primary support point is backed up with supporting details, examples, or facts.
- ☐ The support is arranged in a logical order.
- ☐ The concluding sentence reminds readers of my main point and makes an observation.
- ☐ The title reinforces the main point.
- ☐ All the sentences are complete, consisting of a subject and verb, and expressing a complete thought.
- ☐ The draft is properly formatted:
  - My name, my instructor's name, the course, and the date appear in the upper left corner.
  - The first sentence of the paragraph is indented, and the text is double-spaced (for easier revision).
- ☐ I have followed any other formatting guidelines provided by my instructor.

Write Topic Sentences, and Draft the Body of the Essay

When you start to draft your essay, use your outline to write complete sentences for your primary support points. These sentences will serve as the topic sentences for the body paragraphs of your essay.

As you write support for your topic sentences, refer back to your outline, where you listed supporting details. Turn these supporting details into complete sentences, and add more support if necessary. (Prewriting techniques can help here; see Chapter 2.) Don't let yourself get stalled if you are having trouble with one word or sentence. Just keep writing. Remember that a draft is a first try; you will have time later to improve it.

Write an Introduction

The introduction to your essay captures your readers' interest and presents the main point. Ask yourself: How can I sell my essay to readers? You need to market your main point.

BASICS OF A GOOD INTRODUCTION

- It should catch readers' attention.
- It should present the thesis statement of the essay, usually in the first or the last sentence of an introductory paragraph.
- It should give readers a clear idea of what the essay will cover.

Here are some common kinds of introductions that spark readers' interest.

1. **Open with a quotation.** A good, short quotation definitely gets people interested. It must lead naturally into your main point, however, and not be there just for effect. If you start with a quotation, make sure you tell the reader who the speaker is.

2. **Give an example, or tell a story.** People like stories, so opening an essay with a brief story or example often draws readers in.

3. **Start with a surprising fact or idea.** Surprises capture people's interest. The more unexpected and surprising something is, the more likely people are to notice it.

4. **Offer a strong opinion or position.** The stronger the opinion, the more likely it is that your readers will pay attention. Don't write wimpy introductions. Make your point and shout it!

5. **Ask a question.** A question needs an answer, so if you start your introduction with a question, your readers will need to read on to get the answer.

Write a Conclusion

When they have finished the body of their essay, some writers believe their work is done—but it isn't *quite* finished. Remember that people usually remember best what they see, hear, or read last. Use your concluding paragraph to drive your main point home one final time. Make sure your conclusion has the same energy as the rest of the essay, if not more.

BASICS OF A GOOD ESSAY CONCLUSION

- It refers back to the main point.
- It sums up what has been covered in the essay.
- It makes a further observation or point.

In general, a good conclusion creates a sense of completion. It brings readers back to where they started, but it also shows them how far they have come.

One of the best ways to end an essay is to refer directly to something in the introduction. If you asked a question, re-ask and answer it. If you started a story, finish it. If you used a quote, use another one—maybe a quote by the same person or maybe one by another person on the same topic. Or, use some of the same words you used in your introduction.

Title Your Essay

Even if your title is the *last* part of the essay you write, it is the *first* thing readers read. Use your title to get your readers' attention and to tell them, in a brief way, what your paper is about. Use vivid, strong, specific words.

BASICS OF A GOOD ESSAY TITLE

- It makes people want to read the essay.
- It hints at the main point (thesis statement), but it does not repeat it.

One way to find a good title is to consider the type of essay you are writing. If you are writing an argument, state your position in your title. If you are telling your readers how to do something, try using the term *steps* or *how to* in the title. This way, your readers will know immediately not only what you are writing about but how you will discuss it.

NOTE: Center your title at the top of the page before the first paragraph. Do not put quotation marks around it or underline it.

Sample Student Essay

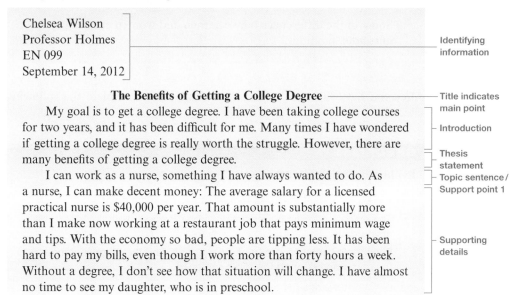

Chelsea Wilson
Professor Holmes
EN 099
September 14, 2012

Identifying information

The Benefits of Getting a College Degree

Title indicates main point

My goal is to get a college degree. I have been taking college courses for two years, and it has been difficult for me. Many times I have wondered if getting a college degree is really worth the struggle. However, there are many benefits of getting a college degree.

Introduction

Thesis statement

I can work as a nurse, something I have always wanted to do. As a nurse, I can make decent money: The average salary for a licensed practical nurse is $40,000 per year. That amount is substantially more than I make now working at a restaurant job that pays minimum wage and tips. With the economy so bad, people are tipping less. It has been hard to pay my bills, even though I work more than forty hours a week. Without a degree, I don't see how that situation will change. I have almost no time to see my daughter, who is in preschool.

Topic sentence / Support point 1

Supporting details

Topic sentence/
Support point 2

Supporting
details

Topic sentence/
Support point 3

Supporting
details

Conclusion

   I didn't get serious about getting a degree until I became a mother. Then, I realized I wanted more for my daughter than I had growing up. I also wanted to have time to raise her properly and keep her safe. She is a good girl, but she sees crime and violence around her. I want to get her away from danger, and I want to show her that there are better ways to live. Getting a college degree will help me do that.

   The most important benefit of getting a college degree is that it will show me that I can achieve something hard. My life is moving in a good direction, and I am proud of myself. My daughter will be proud of me, too. I want to be a good role model for her as she grows up.

   Because of these benefits, I want to get a college degree. It pays well, it will give my daughter and me a better life, and I will be proud of myself.

WRITING ASSIGNMENT   Essay

Write a draft essay using the material you have developed up to this point or working with one of the following thesis statements. If you choose one of the thesis statements below, you may want to modify it to fit what you want to say.

Taking care of a sick (child/parent/spouse/friend) can test even the most patient person.

Being a good _____ requires _____.

Doing _____ gave me a great deal of pride in myself.

A good long-term relationship involves flexibility and compromise.

Some of the differences between men and women create misunderstandings.

After you have finished writing your draft essay, complete the following checklist.

CHECKLIST

Evaluating Your Draft Essay

☐ A clear, confident thesis statement states my main point.

☐ The primary support points are now topic sentences that support the main point.

☐ Each topic sentence is part of a paragraph, and the other sentences in the paragraph support the topic sentence.

- [ ] The support is arranged in a logical order.
- [ ] The introduction will interest readers.
- [ ] The conclusion reinforces my main point and makes an additional observation.
- [ ] The title reinforces the main point.
- [ ] All the sentences are complete, consisting of a subject and verb, and expressing a complete thought.
- [ ] The draft is properly formatted:
  - My name, my instructor's name, the course, and the date appear in the upper left corner.
  - The first sentence of each paragraph is indented, and the text is double-spaced (for easier revision).
  - The pages are numbered.
- [ ] I have followed any other formatting guidelines provided by my instructor.

Do not think about your draft anymore—for the moment. Give yourself some time away from it, at least a few hours and preferably a day or two. Taking a break will allow you to return to your writing later with a fresher eye and more energy for revision, resulting in a better piece of writing—and a better grade. After your break, you will be ready to take the next step: revising your draft.

Revising Paragraphs and Essays

When you finish a draft, you probably wish that you were at the end: You don't want to have to look at it again. But a draft is just the first whole version, a rough cut; it is not the best you can do to represent yourself and your ideas. After taking a break, you need to look at the draft with fresh eyes to revise and edit it.

Revising is making your ideas clearer, stronger, and more convincing. When revising, you are evaluating how well you have made your point.

Editing is finding and correcting problems with grammar, word usage, punctuation, and capitalization. When editing, you are evaluating the words, phrases, and sentences you have used.

Most writers find it difficult to revise and edit well if they try to do both at once. It is easier to solve idea-level problems first (by revising) and then to correct smaller, word-level ones (by editing).

TIPS FOR REVISING YOUR WRITING

- Wait a few hours or, if possible, a couple of days before starting to revise.

- Read your draft aloud, and listen for places where the writing seems weak or unclear.

- Read critically and ask yourself questions, as if you were reading through someone else's eyes. (For more on reading critically, see Chapter 1.)

- Write notes about changes to make. For small things, like adding a transition (p. 56), you can make the change on the draft. For other things, like adding or getting rid of an idea or reordering your support points, make a note in the margin.

- Get help from a tutor at the writing center, or get feedback from a friend (see page 61 for information on peer review).

Even the best writers do not get everything right the first time. So, if you finish reading your draft and have not found anything that could be better, either you are not reading carefully enough or you are not asking the right questions. Use the following checklist to help you make your writing better.

CHECKLIST

Revising Your Writing

- [ ] If someone else just read my topic sentence or thesis statement, what would he or she think the paper is about? Would the main point make a lasting impression? What would I need to do to make it more interesting?

- [ ] Does each support point really relate to my main point? What more could I say about the topic so that someone else will see it my way? Is any of what I have written weak? If so, should I delete it?

- [ ] What about the way the ideas are arranged? Should I change the order so that the writing makes more sense or has more effect on a reader?

- [ ] What about the ending? Does it just droop and fade away? How could I make it better?

- [ ] If, before reading my paragraph or essay, someone knew nothing about the topic or disagreed with my position, would what I have written be enough for him or her to understand the material or be convinced by my argument?

You may need to read what you have written several times before deciding what changes would improve it. Remember to consider your audience and your purpose and to focus on three main areas: unity, detail, and coherence.

Revise for Unity

Unity in writing means that all the points you make are related to your main point; they are *unified* in support of it. As you draft a paragraph or an essay, you may detour from your main point without even being aware of it, as the writer of the following paragraph did with the underlined sentences. (The main point in the paragraph has been double-underlined.)

> If you want to drive like an elderly person, use a cell phone while driving. A group of researchers from the University of Utah tested the reaction times of two groups of people—those between the ages of sixty-five to seventy-four and those who were eighteen to twenty-five—in a variety of driving tasks. All tasks were done with hands-free cell phones. That part of the study surprised me because I thought the main problem was using only one hand to drive. I hardly ever drive with two hands, even when I'm not talking to anyone. Among other results, braking time for both groups slowed by 18 percent. A related result is that the number of rear-end collisions doubled. The study determined that the younger drivers were paying as much—or more—attention to their phone conversations as they were to what was going on around them on the road. The elderly drivers also experienced longer reaction times and more accidents, pushing most of them into the category of dangerous driver. This study makes a good case for turning off the phone when you buckle up.

Detours such as the underlined sentences in the example weaken your writing because readers' focus is shifted from your main point. As you revise, check to make sure your paragraph or essay has unity.

Revise for Detail and Support

When you revise a paper, look carefully at the support you have developed. Will readers have enough information to understand and be convinced by the main point?

In the margin or between the lines of your draft (which should be double-spaced), note ideas that seem weak or unclear. As you revise, build up your support by adding more details.

What makes them act this way?

Provide an example of a riot?

Why do parents turn violent? Example?

In the example below, the main point has been double-underlined and notes have been made in the margins to suggest revision ideas for improved support.

<u><u>Sports fans can turn from normal people into destructive maniacs.</u></u> After big wins, a team's fans sometimes riot. Police have to be brought in. Even in school sports, parents of the players can become violent. People get so involved watching the game that they lose control of themselves and are dangerous.

Revise for Coherence

Coherence in writing means that all your support connects to form a whole. In other words, you have provided enough "glue" for readers to see how one point leads to another.

A good way to improve coherence is to use **transitions**—words, phrases, and sentences that connect your ideas so that your writing moves smoothly from one point to the next. The table below shows some common transitions and what they are used for.

In the paragraph that follows, the transitions have been underlined.

It is not difficult to get organized—<u>even though</u> it takes discipline to stay organized. All you need to do is follow a few simple ideas. You must decide what your priorities are and do these tasks first. <u>For example</u>, you should ask yourself every day: What is the most important task I have to accomplish? <u>Then</u>, make the time to do it. To be organized, you <u>also</u> need a personal system for keeping track of things. Making lists, keeping records, and using a schedule help you remember what tasks you need to do. <u>Finally</u>, it is a good idea not to let belongings and obligations stack up. Get rid of possessions you do not need, put items away every time you are done using them, and do not take on more responsibilities than you can handle. Getting organized is not a mystery; it is just good sense.

Common Transitional Words and Phrases

INDICATING SPACE

above	below	near	to the right
across	beside	next to	to the side
at the bottom	beyond	opposite	under
at the top	farther/further	over	where
behind	inside	to the left	

INDICATING TIME

after	eventually	meanwhile	soon
as	finally	next	then
at last	first	now	when
before	last	second	while
during	later	since	

INDICATING IMPORTANCE

above all	in fact	more important	most important
best	in particular	most	worst
especially			

SIGNALING EXAMPLES

for example	for instance	for one thing	one reason

SIGNALING ADDITIONS

additionally	and	as well as	in addition
also	another	furthermore	moreover

SIGNALING CONTRAST

although	however	nevertheless	still
but	in contrast	on the other hand	yet
even though	instead		

SIGNALING CAUSES OR RESULTS

as a result	finally	so	therefore
because			

Another way to give your writing coherence is to repeat a **key word**—a word that is directly related to your main point. For example, in the paragraph on page 56, the writer repeats the word *organized* several times. Repetition of a key word is a good way to keep your readers focused on your main point, but make sure you don't overdo it.

Sample Student Paragraph: Revised

Compare the revised paragraph below to the original draft on page 48.

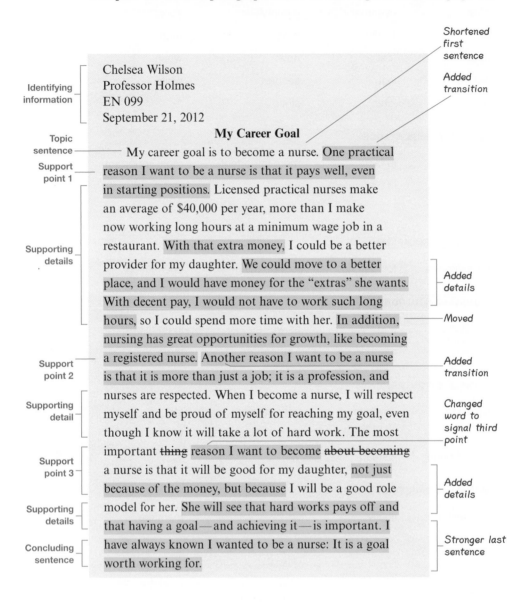

Identifying information

Topic sentence

Support point 1

Supporting details

Support point 2

Supporting detail

Support point 3

Supporting details

Concluding sentence

Shortened first sentence

Added transition

Chelsea Wilson
Professor Holmes
EN 099
September 21, 2012

My Career Goal

My career goal is to become a nurse. One practical reason I want to be a nurse is that it pays well, even in starting positions. Licensed practical nurses make an average of $40,000 per year, more than I make now working long hours at a minimum wage job in a restaurant. With that extra money, I could be a better provider for my daughter. We could move to a better place, and I would have money for the "extras" she wants. With decent pay, I would not have to work such long hours, so I could spend more time with her. In addition, nursing has great opportunities for growth, like becoming a registered nurse. Another reason I want to be a nurse is that it is more than just a job; it is a profession, and nurses are respected. When I become a nurse, I will respect myself and be proud of myself for reaching my goal, even though I know it will take a lot of hard work. The most important ~~thing~~ reason I want to become ~~about becoming~~ a nurse is that it will be good for my daughter, not just because of the money, but because I will be a good role model for her. She will see that hard works pays off and that having a goal—and achieving it—is important. I have always known I wanted to be a nurse: It is a goal worth working for.

Added details

Moved

Added transition

Changed word to signal third point

Added details

Stronger last sentence

......

WRITING ASSIGNMENT   Paragraph

Revise the draft paragraph you wrote earlier in this chapter. After revising your draft, complete the following checklist.

CHECKLIST

Evaluating Your Revised Paragraph

☐ My topic sentence is confident, and my main point is clear.

☐ My ideas are detailed, specific, and organized logically.

☐ My ideas flow smoothly from one to the next.

☐ This paragraph fulfills the original assignment.

☐ I am ready to turn in this paragraph for a grade.

☐ This paragraph is the best I can do.

After you have finished revising your paragraph, you are ready to edit it for grammar, word use, punctuation, and capitalization.

Sample Student Essay: Revised

Compare the revised essay below to the original draft on pages 51–52.

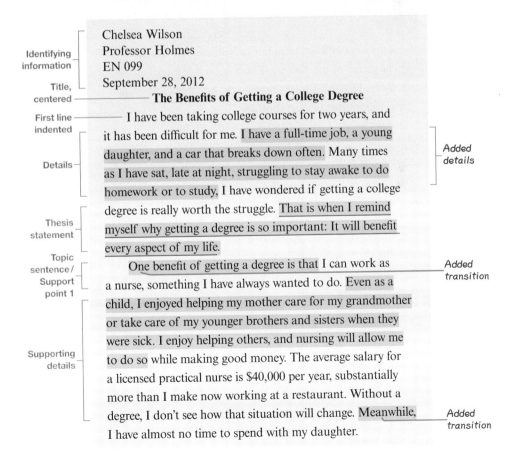

Identifying information	Chelsea Wilson
	Professor Holmes
	EN 099
Title, centered	September 28, 2012
	The Benefits of Getting a College Degree
First line indented	I have been taking college courses for two years, and
	it has been difficult for me. I have a full-time job, a young
Details	daughter, and a car that breaks down often. Many times
	as I have sat, late at night, struggling to stay awake to do
	homework or to study, I have wondered if getting a college
	degree is really worth the struggle. That is when I remind
Thesis statement	myself why getting a degree is so important: It will benefit
	every aspect of my life.
Topic sentence / Support point 1	One benefit of getting a degree is that I can work as
	a nurse, something I have always wanted to do. Even as a
	child, I enjoyed helping my mother care for my grandmother
	or take care of my younger brothers and sisters when they
	were sick. I enjoy helping others, and nursing will allow me
Supporting details	to do so while making good money. The average salary for
	a licensed practical nurse is $40,000 per year, substantially
	more than I make now working at a restaurant. Without a
	degree, I don't see how that situation will change. Meanwhile,
	I have almost no time to spend with my daughter.

Added details

Added transition

Added transition

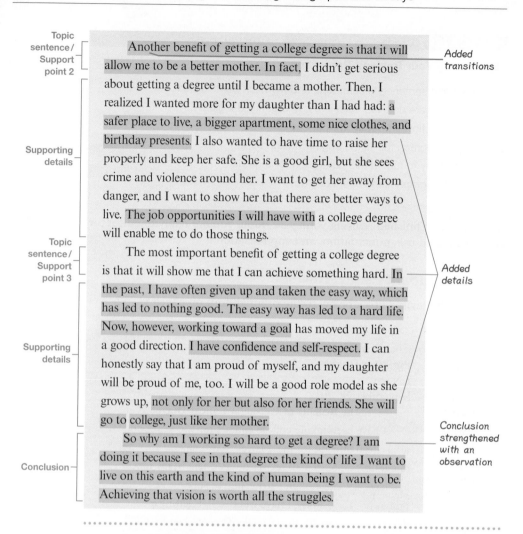

Topic sentence/ Support point 2

Supporting details

Topic sentence/ Support point 3

Supporting details

Conclusion

Added transitions

Added details

Conclusion strengthened with an observation

Another benefit of getting a college degree is that it will allow me to be a better mother. In fact, I didn't get serious about getting a degree until I became a mother. Then, I realized I wanted more for my daughter than I had had: a safer place to live, a bigger apartment, some nice clothes, and birthday presents. I also wanted to have time to raise her properly and keep her safe. She is a good girl, but she sees crime and violence around her. I want to get her away from danger, and I want to show her that there are better ways to live. The job opportunities I will have with a college degree will enable me to do those things.

The most important benefit of getting a college degree is that it will show me that I can achieve something hard. In the past, I have often given up and taken the easy way, which has led to nothing good. The easy way has led to a hard life. Now, however, working toward a goal has moved my life in a good direction. I have confidence and self-respect. I can honestly say that I am proud of myself, and my daughter will be proud of me, too. I will be a good role model as she grows up, not only for her but also for her friends. She will go to college, just like her mother.

So why am I working so hard to get a degree? I am doing it because I see in that degree the kind of life I want to live on this earth and the kind of human being I want to be. Achieving that vision is worth all the struggles.

WRITING ASSIGNMENT   Essay

Revise the draft essay you wrote earlier in this chapter. After revising your draft, complete the following checklist.

CHECKLIST

Evaluating Your Revised Essay

- ☐ My thesis statement is confident, and my main point is clear.
- ☐ My ideas are detailed, specific, and organized logically.
- ☐ My ideas flow smoothly from one to the next.
- ☐ This essay fulfills the original assignment.
- ☐ I am ready to turn in this essay for a grade.
- ☐ This essay is the best I can do.

After you have revised your writing to make the ideas clear and strong, you need to edit it for grammar, word use, punctuation, and capitalization.

Peer Reviewing

Peer review—when students exchange drafts and comment on one another's work—is one of the best ways to get help with revising. Other students can often see things that you might not—parts that are good and parts that need to be strengthened or clarified.

If you are working with one other student, read each other's papers and write down a few comments. If you are working in a small group, you may want to have writers take turns reading their papers aloud. Group members can make notes while listening and then offer comments to the writer that will help improve the paper.

BASICS OF USEFUL FEEDBACK

- It is given in a positive way.
- It offers specific suggestions.
- It may be given in writing or orally.

Often, it is useful for the writer to give the person or people providing feedback a few questions to focus on as they read or listen.

CHECKLIST

Questions for Peer Reviewers

- ☐ What is the main point?
- ☐ Can I do anything to make my opening more interesting?
- ☐ Do I have enough support for my main point? Where could I use more?
- ☐ Where could I use more details?
- ☐ Are there places where you have to stop and reread something to understand it? If so, where?
- ☐ Do I give my reader clues as to where a new point starts? Does one point "flow" smoothly to the next?
- ☐ What about my conclusion? Does it just fade out? How could I make my point more forcefully?
- ☐ Where else could the paper be better? What would you do if it were your paper?
- ☐ If you were going to be graded on this paper, would you turn it in as is? If not, why not?
- ☐ What other comments or suggestions do you have?

5

Narration

Writing That Tells Important Stories

Understand What Narration Is

Narration is writing that tells the story of an event or an experience.

Four Basics of Good Narration

1. It has a message you want to share with readers (your main point).
2. It includes all the major events of the story (primary support).
3. It brings the story to life with details about the major events (secondary support).
4. It presents the events in a clear order, usually according to when they happened.

In the following paragraph, the numbers and colors correspond to the Four Basics of Good Narration.

4 Events in time order

1 Last year, a writing assignment that I hated produced the best writing I have done. **2** When my English teacher told us that our assignment would be to do a few hours of community service and write about it, I was furious. **3** I am a single mother, I work full-time, and I am going to school: Isn't that enough? **2** The next day, I spoke to my teacher during her office hours and told her that I was already so busy that I could hardly make time for homework, never mind housework. My own life was too full to help with any-one else's life. **3** She said that she understood perfectly and that the majority of her students had lives as full as mine. Then, she explained that the service assignment was just for four hours and that other students had enjoyed both doing the assignment and writing about their experiences. She said they were all surprised and that I would be, too. **2** After talking with her, I decided to ac-cept my fate. The next week, I went to the Community Service Club, and was set up to spend a few hours at an adult day-care center near where I live. A few weeks later, I went to the Creative Care Center in Cocoa Beach, not knowing what to expect. **3** I found friendly, approachable people who had so many stories to tell about their long, full lives. **2** The next thing I knew, I was tak-ing notes because I was interested in these people: **3** their mar-riages, life during the Depression, the wars they fought in, their children, their joys and sorrows. I felt as if I was experiencing ev-erything they lived while they shared their history with me. **2** When it came time to write about my experience, I had more than enough to write about: **3** I wrote the stories of the many wonder-ful elderly people I had talked with. **2** I got an A on the paper, and beyond that accomplishment, I made friends whom I will visit on my own, not because of an assignment, but because I value them.

You can use narration in many practical situations.

COLLEGE	In a lab course, you are asked to tell what happened in an experiment.
WORK	Something goes wrong at work, and you are asked to explain to your boss — in writing — what happened.
EVERYDAY LIFE	In a letter of complaint about service you received, you need to tell what happened that upset you.

In college, the word *narration* probably will not appear in writing as-signments. Instead, an assignment might ask you to *describe* the events, *re-port* what happened, or *retell* what happened. Words or phrases that call for an *account of events* are situations that require narration.

PARAGRAPHS VS. ESSAYS IN NARRATION

For more on the important features of narration, see the Four Basics of Good Narration on page 62.

Paragraph Form

Topic sentence

Support 1 (first major event)

Support 2 (second major event)

Support 3 (third major event)

Support Concluding sentence

My first day at my new job was nearly a disaster. First, a traffic jam from highway construction caused me to be a half hour late. I had left myself plenty of time for the commute, but because of the traffic backup, it took me nearly an hour to travel seven miles. At one point, I tried a detour to avoid traffic, but I ended up getting lost. By the time I finally pulled into the employee parking lot, I was already full of stress. After I arrived in the office, I discovered that I would have to fill in for a sick worker whose job I was not familiar with. I had been trained in accounts payable, while my sick colleague worked in accounts receivable. Although I had some understanding of his job, I was worried about making mistakes and had to ask coworkers a lot of questions, which took a lot of time. For example, I estimate that I spent a half hour on a billing procedure that would take an experienced worker five minutes. Near the end of the day, my computer broke down, erasing two documents that I had been working on. One was a small set of file labels, but the other was a detailed summary of the day's billings. At this point, I wanted to put my head down on my desk and cry. Seeing my distress, my supervisor came by and kindly said, "You have had a long, hard day and done great work. Why don't you go home and make a fresh start tomorrow?" I was grateful for her kindness, and I came around to thinking that if I could handle this type of day on the new job, I could handle just about any day.

Main Point: Often, narrower for a paragraph than for an essay: While the topic sentence (paragraph) is focused on just one workday, the thesis statement (essay) considers a season-long internship.

Major Events Supporting the Main Point

Details about the Events: Usually, 1 to 3 sentences per event for paragraphs and 3 to 8 sentences per event for essays.

Conclusion

Essay Form

Several of my friends question whether summer internships are really worthwhile, especially if the pay is low or nonexistent. However, the right internship definit~~...~~ **Thesis statement** professionally in the long run even ~~...~~ financially in the short run. The proof is in my own summer marketing internship, which made me a far more confident and skilled worker.

During the first two weeks of the internship, I received thorough training in every part of my job. For example, my immediate superviso~~...~~ **Topic sentence 1 (first major event)** full days going over everything I woul~~...~~ to help with e-mail campaigns, onlin~~...~~ efforts, and other promotions. She even had me draft a promotional e-mail for a new product and gave me feedback about how to make the message clearer and more appealing. I also spent a lot of time with other staffers, who taught me everything from how to use the photocopier and printers to how to pull together marketing and sales materials

for executive meetings. Most impressive, the president of the company took some time out of a busy afternoon to answer my questions about how he got started in his career and what he sees as the keys to success in the marketi~~...~~ **Topic sentence 2 (second major event)** explained to a friend, I got a real "i~~...~~ of the company and its leadership.

Next, I got hands-on experience with listening to customers and addressing their needs. Specifically, I sat in on meetings with new clients and listened to them describe products and services they would like the company's help in promoting. They also discussed the message they would like to get across about their businesses. After the meetings, I sat in on brainstorming sessions with other staffers in which we came up with as many ideas as we could about campaigns to address the clients' needs. At first, I didn't think anyone would care about my ideas, but others listened to them respectfully and even ended up including some of

them in the marketing plans that were sent back to the clients. Later, I learned that some of my ideas would be included in the actual promotional campaigns.

By summer's end, I had advanced my skills so much that I was asked to return next summer. My s~~...~~ **Topic sentence 3 (third major event)** told me that she was pleased not only with all I ha~~...~~ about marketing but also with the responsibility I~~...~~ every aspect of my job. I did not roll my eyes about having to make photocopies or help at the reception desk, nor did I seem intimidated by bigger, more meaningful tasks. Although I'm not guaranteed a full-time job at the company after graduation, I think my chances are good. Even if I don't end up working there long term, I am very grateful for how the job has helped me grow.

In the end, the greatest benefit of the internship might be the confidence it gave me. I have learned that no matter how challenging the task before me—at work or in real life—I can succeed at it by getting the right information and **Concluding paragraph** anything unfamiliar, working effectively with others, and truly dedicating myself to doing my best. My time this past summer was definitely well spent.

Main Point in Narration

In narration, the **main point** is what is important about the story—to you and to your readers. The topic sentence (paragraph) or thesis statement (essay) usually includes the topic and the main point the writer wants to make about the topic. Let's look at a topic sentence first.

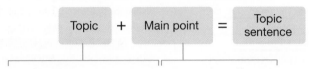

My first day at my new job was nearly a disaster.

Remember that a topic for an essay can be a little broader than one for a paragraph.

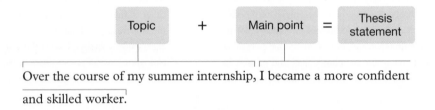

Over the course of my summer internship, I became a more confident and skilled worker.

Whereas the topic sentence is focused on just one work day, the thesis statement considers a season-long internship.

Support in Narration

In narration, **support** demonstrates the main point—what's important about the story.

The paragraph and essay models on pages 64–65 use the topic sentence (paragraph) and thesis statement (essay) from the Main Point section of this chapter. (The thesis statement has been revised slightly.) Both models include the support used in all narration writing—major events backed up by details about the events. In the essay model, however, the major support points (events) are topic sentences for individual paragraphs.

Organization in Narration

Narration usually presents events in the order in which they happened, known as **time (chronological) order**. (For more on time order, see page 42.) As shown in the paragraph and essay models on pages 64–65, a narration starts at the beginning of the story and describes events as they unfolded.

Transitions move readers from one event to the next.

Common Transitions in Narration

after	eventually	meanwhile	since
as	finally	next	soon
at last	first	now	then
before	last	once	when
during	later	second	while

Read and Analyze Narration

After you have read each of the selections below, answer the questions that follow.

Narration in the Real World

Kelly Layland, Registered Nurse

Patient Report

 After graduating from Monroe Community College with an associate's degree, Kelly Layland went on to earn her LPN from Isabella Graham Hart School of Nursing, and her RN from Monroe Community College. As a registered nurse of Rochester General Hospital, Kelly writes brief narratives every day that recount all that goes on with her patients: things that went wrong and things about their treatments that need to be changed. Below is an example of one of Kelly's brief narratives.

Karella Lehmanoff, a two-month-old female infant, is improving steadily. When she was born, her birth weight was 1.3 pounds, but it has increased to 3.1 pounds. Her jaundice has completely disappeared, and her skin has begun to look rosy. Karella's pulse rate is normal for her development, and her resting heart rate has stabilized at about 150 beats per minute. Lung development was a big concern because of Karella's premature birth, but her lungs are now fully developed and largely functional. Dr. Lansing saw Karella at 1 P.M. and pronounced her in good condition. The parents were encouraged, and so am I. The prognosis for little Karella gets better with each day.

1. Double-underline the **main point** of the narration.
2. Underline the **major events**.
3. What order of organization does Kelly use?

Student Narration Paragraph

Jelani Lynch

My Turnaround

 Jelani Lynch graduated from Cambridge College / Year Up in 2009 with a degree in information technology. Now, he runs the video production company J / L visual media. As a writer, he says he is interested in exploring "issues that affect the community and the disparities that continue to affect the world." Reflecting on what motivated him to write this essay, Jelani said "I wrote this after I had just begun to get my life on track. I felt that my struggles needed to be publicized so my mistakes are not repeated by the people who read it."

Before my big turnaround, my life was headed in the wrong direction. I grew up in the city and had a typical sad story: broken home, not much money, gangs, and drugs. In this world, few positive male role models are available. I played the game "Street Life": running the streets, stealing bikes, robbing people, carrying a gun, and selling drugs. The men in my neighborhood did not have regular jobs; they got their money outside the system. No one except my mother thought school was worth much. I had a history of poor school performance, a combination of not showing up and not doing any work when I did. My pattern of failure in that area was pretty strong. When I was seventeen, though, things got really bad. I was arrested for possession of crack cocaine. I was kicked out of school for good. During this time, I realized that my life was not going the way I wanted it to be. I was headed nowhere, except a life of crime, violence, and possibly early death. I knew that way of life, because I was surrounded by people who had chosen that direction. I did not want to go there anymore. When I made that decision, my life started to change. First, I met Shawn Brown, a man who had had the same kind of life I did. He got out of that life, though, by graduating from high school and college and getting a good job. He has a house, a wife, and children, along with great clothes. Shawn became my role model, showing me that with honesty, integrity, and hard work I could live a much better life. Since meeting Shawn, I have turned my life around. I started taking school seriously and graduated from high school, something I thought I would never do. Working with Shawn, I have read books and learned I enjoy writing. I have met the mayor of Boston and got a summer job at the State House. I have been part of an educational video and had many opportunities to meet and work with people who are successful. Now, I am a mentor with Diamond Educators, and I work with other young, urban males to give them a role model and help them make good choices. Now, I have a bright future with goals and plans. I have turned my life around and know I will be a success.

1. Double-underline the **topic sentence**.
2. What is important about the story?
3. Underline the **major events**.
4. Circle the **transitions**.
5. Does Jelani's paragraph follow the Four Basics of Good Narration (p. 62)?

Vocabulary development

integrity: honesty; having a sound moral code

mentor: a counselor, a teacher, an adviser

Professional Narration Essay

Amy Tan

Fish Cheeks

Amy Tan was born in Oakland, California, in 1952, several years after her mother and father emigrated from China. She studied at San Jose City College and later San Jose State University, receiving a B.A. with a double major in English and linguistics, and in 1973, an M.A. in linguistics. In 1989, Tan published her first novel, *The Joy Luck Club*, which was nominated for the National Book Award and the National Book Critics Circle Award. Tan's other books include *The Kitchen God's Wife* (1991) and *Saving Fish from Drowning* (2005).

In the following essay, Tan uses narration to describe an experience that taught her an important lesson.

1   I fell in love with the minister's son the winter I turned fourteen. He was not Chinese, but as white as Mary in the manger. For Christmas I prayed for this blond-haired boy, Robert, and a slim new American nose.

When I found out that my parents had invited the minister's family over 2 for Christmas dinner, I cried. What would Robert think of our shabby Chinese Christmas? What would he think of our noisy Chinese relatives who lacked proper American manners? What terrible disappointment would he feel upon seeing not a roasted turkey and sweet potatoes but Chinese food?

On Christmas Eve I saw that my mother had outdone herself in creat- 3 ing a strange menu. She was pulling black veins out of the backs of fleshy prawns. The kitchen was littered with appalling mounds of raw food: A slimy rock cod with bulging eyes that pleaded not to be thrown into a pan of hot oil. Tofu, which looked like stacked wedges of rubbery white sponges. A bowl soaking dried fungus back to life. A plate of squid, their backs criss-crossed with knife markings so they resembled bicycle tires.

And then they arrived—the minister's family and all my relatives in a 4 clamor of doorbells and rumpled Christmas packages. Robert grunted hello, and I pretended he was not worthy of existence.

Dinner threw me into despair. My relatives licked the ends of their chop- 5 sticks and reached across the table, dipping them into the dozen or so plates of food. Robert and his family waited patiently for platters to be passed to them. My relatives murmured with pleasure when my mother brought out the whole steamed fish. Robert grimaced. Then my father poked his chop-sticks just below the fish eye and plucked out the soft meat. "Amy, your fa-vorite," he said, offering me the tender fish cheek. I wanted to disappear.

At the end of the meal my father leaned back and belched loudly, thank- 6 ing my mother for her fine cooking. "It's a polite Chinese custom to show you are satisfied," explained my father to our astonished guests. Robert was looking down at his plate with a reddened face. The minister managed to muster up a quiet burp. I was stunned into silence for the rest of the night.

After everyone had gone, my mother said to me, "You want to be the 7 same as American girls on the outside." She handed me an early gift. It was a miniskirt in beige tweed. "But inside you must always be Chinese. You must be proud you are different. Your only shame is to have shame."

And even though I didn't agree with her then, I knew that she under- 8 stood how much I had suffered during the evening's dinner. It wasn't until many years later—long after I had gotten over my crush on Robert— that I was able to fully appreciate her lesson and the true purpose behind our particular menu. For Christmas Eve that year, she had chosen all my favorite foods.

Vocabulary development

prawns: shrimp or shrimp-like creatures

appalling: horrifying

clamor: noise

murmured: spoke in low tones

belched: burped

1. What is Tan's purpose for writing? Does she achieve it?

2. In your own words, state Tan's **main point**.

3. How has Tan organized her essay? Circle the **transitional words and phrases** that indicate this order.

Write Your Own Narration

Write a narration paragraph or essay on one of the following topics or on one of your own choice. For help, refer to the How to Write Narration checklist below and on page 72.

COLLEGE

- Tell the story of how a teacher made a difference in your life.

- Write about a time when you achieved success or experienced a difficulty in school.

WORK

- Write about a situation or incident that made you decide to leave a job.

- Imagine a successful day at your current or previous job. Then, tell the story of that day, including examples of successes.

EVERYDAY LIFE

- Write about an experience that triggered a strong emotion: happiness, sadness, fear, anger, regret.

- Go to the student government office and find out if there is a community service club that offers short-term assignments. Take one of these assignments, and write about your experience.

CHECKLIST: HOW TO WRITE NARRATION	
STEPS	**DETAILS**
☐ Narrow and explore your topic. See Chapter 2.	• Make the topic more specific. • Prewrite to get ideas about the narrowed topic.
☐ Write a topic sentence (paragraph) or thesis statement (essay). See Chapter 3.	• State what is most important to you about the topic and what you want your readers to understand.
☐ Support your point. See Chapter 3.	• Come up with examples and details to explain your main point to readers.

STEPS	DETAILS
☐ **Write a draft.** See Chapter 4.	• Make a plan that puts events or examples in a logical order. • Include a topic sentence (paragraph) or thesis statement (essay) and all the supporting events, examples, and details.
☐ **Revise your draft.** See Chapter 4.	• Make sure it has *all* the Four Basics of Good Narration. • Make sure you include transitions to move readers smoothly from one event or example to the next.
☐ **Edit your revised draft.** See Chapters 14 through 17.	• Correct errors in grammar, spelling, word use, and punctuation.

6

Illustration

Writing That Gives Examples

Understand What Illustration Is

Illustration is writing that uses examples to support a point.

Four Basics of Good Illustration

1 It has a point.

2 It gives specific examples that show, explain, or prove the point.

3 It gives details to support the examples.

4 It uses enough examples to get the point across to the reader.

In the following paragraph, the numbers and colors correspond to the Four Basics of Good Illustration.

1 Many people would like to serve their communities or help with causes that they believe in, but they do not have much time and do not know what to do. Now, the Internet provides people with ways to help that do not take much time or money. **2** Web sites now make it convenient to donate online. With a few clicks, an organization of your choice can receive your donation or money from a sponsoring advertiser. For example, if you are interested in helping rescue unwanted and abandoned animals, you can go to www .theanimalrescuesite.com. **3** When you click as instructed, a sponsoring advertiser will make a donation to help provide food and care for the 27 million animals in shelters. Also, a portion of any

4 Enough examples to get the point across to the reader

✓ LearningCurve For extra practice in the skills covered in this chapter, visit: bedfordstmartins.com/rwinteractive.

73

money you spend in the site's online store will go to providing animal care. **2** If you want to help fight world hunger, go to www.thehungersite.com **3** and click daily to have sponsor fees directed to hungry people in more than seventy countries via the Mercy Corps, Feeding America, and Millennium Promise. Each year, hundreds of millions of cups of food are distributed to one billion hungry people around the world. **2** Other examples of click-to-give sites are www.thechildhealthsite.com, www.theliteracysite.com, and www.breastcancersite.com. **3** Like the animal-rescue and hunger sites, these other sites have click-to-give links, online stores that direct a percentage of sales income to charity, and links to help you learn about causes you are interested in. One hundred percent of the sponsors' donations go to the charities, and you can give with a click every single day. Since I have found out about these sites, I go to at least one of them every day. **1** I have learned a lot about various problems, and every day, I feel as if I have helped a little.

It is hard to explain anything without using examples, so you use illustration in almost every communication situation.

COLLEGE	An exam question asks you to explain and give examples of a concept.
WORK	Your boss asks you to tell her what office equipment needs to be replaced and why.
EVERYDAY LIFE	You complain to your landlord that the building superintendent is not doing his job. The landlord asks for examples.

In college, the words *illustration* and *illustrate* may not appear in writing assignments. Instead, you might be asked to *give examples of _____* or to *be specific about _____*. Regardless of an assignment's wording, to be clear and effective, most types of writing require specific examples. Include them whenever they help you make your point.

Main Point in Illustration

In illustration, the **main point** is the message you want your readers to receive and understand. The topic sentence (in a paragraph) or thesis statement (in an essay) usually includes the topic and the main point the writer wants to make about the topic. Let's look at a topic sentence first.

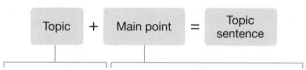

Home health aides provide vital services to the elderly.

Remember that a thesis statement for an essay can be a little broader than a paragraph topic.

Demand for elder-care health workers is increasing rapidly.

Whereas the topic sentence is focused on just home health aides, the thesis statement considers elder-care careers in general.

Support in Illustration

The paragraph and essay models on pages 76–77 use the topic sentence (paragraph) and thesis statement (essay) from the Main Point section of this chapter. Both models include the **support** used in all illustration writing: examples backed up by details about the examples. In the essay model, however, the major support points (examples) are topic sentences for individual paragraphs.

To generate good detailed examples, use one or more of the prewriting techniques discussed in Chapter 2. First, write down all the examples that come into your mind. Then, review your examples, and choose the ones that will best communicate your point to your readers.

PARAGRAPHS VS. ESSAYS IN ILLUSTRATION

For more on the important features of narration, see the Four Basics of Good Illustration on page 73.

Paragraph Form

Main Point: Often, narrower for a paragraph than for an essay: While the topic sentence (paragraph) is focused on just home health aides, the thesis statement (essay) considers elder-care careers in general.

Topic sentence

Home health aides provide vital services to the elderly. First, they see to their clients' nutritional and personal-care needs. For instance, they often shop for and prepare meals, following any dietary restrictions clients may have. In addition, they may help clients get in and out of bed, bathe, dress, and accomplish other grooming tasks. Second, home health aides may assist with medical care. For example, they may check clients' vital signs and report any problems to the hospital or to a case manager. Specially trained aides may oversee the operation of medical equipment, such as ventilators; provide therapeutic massage; or assist with physical therapy. Most important, they provide companionship and emotional support. The simple presence of a home health aide is a comfort to clients, but aides who take the time to read to or have conversations with clients are especially valued. Additionally, health aides provide an important link between patients and their families, keeping relatives up to date about the patients' status and about any special needs that may arise. Aside from supplying key information, these updates let family members know that their loved one is in good hands. The bottom line is that for those who are interested in both the personal and the technical sides of health care, a job as a home health aide can be a good start.

Support 1 (first example)

Support 2 (second example)

Support 3 (third example)

Concluding sentence

Examples Supporting the Main Point

Details about the Examples: Usually, 1 to 3 sentences per example for paragraphs and 3 to 8 sentences per example for essays.

Conclusion

Essay Form

1

During these difficult economic times, many students are looking to pursue careers in expanding fields with good long-ter [**Thesis statement**] One field that they should seriou is elder care. Because the U.S. population is aging, demand for workers who specialize in the health of the elderly is increasing rapidly.

One set of workers in great demand consists of physical therapists, who help elderly patients improve their mobility and retain their independence. Some of these therap [**Topic sentence 1 (first example)**] at hospitals or nursing facilities, ot or private offices. Regardless of where they work, they provide a variety of services to elderly patients, from helping stroke sufferers relearn how to walk and perform other daily activities to showing others how to live a more active life. Physical therapists can also help patients injured in falls reduce their reliance on painkillers, which can become less effective over time and in certain

2

cases even addictive. According to the U.S. Department of Labor, employment of physical therapists will grow by 30 percent over the next ten years, largely because of the increasing number of elderly Americans.

Also in demand are nutritionists who specialize in older people's dietary needs. These professionals may plan m [**Topic sentence 2 (second example)**] provide nutrition advice for hospitals homes, and other institutions, or t counsel individual patients on how to eat more healthfully or on how to prepare meals that meet certain dietary restrictions. For instance, elderly patients suffering from heart disease may need to eat foods that are low in salt and saturated fat. Other patients might have to avoid foods that interfere with the absorption of certain medications. Although the market for nutritionists is not expected to grow as quickly as that for physical therapists, it is

3

projected to increase steadily as the population continues to age.

The highest-demand workers are those who provide at-home health care to the elderly. One subset of these workers cons [**Topic sentence 3 (third example)**] nurses, who often provide follow-patients are released from a hosp medical facility. These nurses help patients transition from an institutional setting while making sure they continue to receive high-quality care. For instance, they track patients' vital signs, administer and monitor medications, and carry out specific tasks required to manage particular diseases. Another subset of home health workers is made up of home health aides, who assist nurses and other professionals with medical care, see to clients' nutritional and personal-care needs, and provide companionship and emotional support. Both home health aides and nurses provide an important link

4

between patients and their families, keeping relatives up to date about the patients' status and about any special needs that may arise. In addition to supplying key information, these updates let family members know that their loved one is in good hands. Because of home health care workers' vital role in serving the expanding elderly population, their employment is expected to grow significantly: on average, 30 to 40 percent over the next ten years.

Given the growing demand for elder-care workers, people pursuing these professions stand an excellent chance of getting jobs with good long-term outlooks. Based on what I have learned about these professions, the [**Concluding paragraph**] candidates are those who have a strong interest in health or medicine, a willingness to work hard to get the necessary qualifications, and, perhaps most important, an ability to connect with and truly care for others.

Organization in Illustration

Illustration often uses **order of importance**, saving the most powerful example for last. (For more on order of importance and time order, see pages 42 and 43.) This strategy is used in the paragraph and essay models on pages 76–77. Or, if the examples are given according to when they happened, it might be organized by **time order**.

Transitions in illustration let readers know that you are introducing an example or moving from one example to another.

Common Transitions in Illustration

also	first, second, and so on	for instance	in addition
another		for one thing/ for another	the most/the least
finally	for example		one example/ another example

Read and Analyze Illustration

After you read each of the selections below, answer the questions that follow.

Illustration in the Real World

Karen Upright, Systems Manager

Memo

After graduating from Florida Community College with an associate's degree, Karen Upright went on to earn her B.S. from Florida State University and her M.B.A. from Purdue University. As a systems manager at Procter & Gamble, Karen writes memos, systems development plans, speeches for presentations, talk sheets to provide background at meetings, and technical design documents, and e-mail. Below is an example of one of Karen's memos.

From: Upright, Karen
Subject: Women's Network: Assignment Planning Matrix

As you know, we have an enrollment goal for 30 percent of our employees to be women, but we are currently at 20 percent. We need to grow our enrollment, but we also need to retain the women currently in the organization. Greg and I met a few weeks ago to determine how to improve assignment planning for the women in our organization. We agreed to use the Assignment Planning Matrix as a starting point. The matrix is a good career-planning tool, with a section on career interests, rated from "highly desirable" to "undesirable." It also contains a section on specific P&G career interests, with sections to describe aspects that make a particular choice desirable or undesirable and a place to give weight to the various career choices. Completing the matrix requires thought as to what course an individual wants to pursue and why. I have reviewed a sample with and provided training to the women in our organization. Each of them has been asked to complete the matrix, meet with her manager to align on content, and submit a final version to her manager. This information can be shared at the next Leadership Team meeting.

This initiative has several objectives:

- Have each member of the network start a long-term plan for her career.

- Use the long-term plan to develop a short-term plan for assignments and competency development.

- Share this information in written form with the immediate manager and section manager of each member of the network, enabling the manager to speak for each woman's career interests and providing a reference point for each member's career goals.

- Enable the Leadership Team to plan assignments within the organization for each member of the network, matching individual goals and interests to organizational goals and needs.

I encourage you to support the women on your teams as they work through the Assignment Planning Matrix over the next few weeks. Please let me know if you have any questions.

1. Double-underline the **main point** of the memo.
2. Karen gives examples about two topics. What are the two topics?
3. What is the purpose of the memo?

Vocabulary development

retain: to keep

matrix: a grid or table

aspects: parts of

align: to be in line or parallel (in this case, to agree)

objectives: goals

Student Illustration Paragraph

Casandra Palmer

Gifts from the Heart

Casandra Palmer graduated from the University of Akron / Wayne College in 2009. After completing her essay "Gifts from the Heart," Casandra submitted it for publication in her campus paper at the encouragement of her instructor. She spent a few days revising the essay and looked to feedback from others to strengthen her points. Casandra enjoys reading inspirational novels and offers this advice to other student writers: "Learn all you can and never give up. Follow your dreams!"

In our home, gift exchanges have always been meaningful items to us. We do not just give things so that everyone has lots of presents. Each item has a purpose, such as a need or something that someone has desired for a long time. Some things have been given that may have made the other person laugh or cry. I remember one Christmas, our daughter Hannah had her boyfriend, who looked a lot like Harry Potter, join us. We wanted to include him, but we did not know him well, so it was hard to know what to give him. We decided to get Hannah a Harry Potter poster and crossed out the name Harry Potter. In place of Harry Potter, we put her boyfriend's name. Everyone thought it was funny, and we were all laughing, including Hannah's boyfriend. It was a personal gift that he knew we had thought about. For some reason, Hannah did not think it was so funny, but she will still remember it. Another meaningful gift came from watching the movie *Titanic* with my other daughter, Tabitha. We both cried hard and hugged each other. She surprised me by getting a necklace that resembled the gem known as "Heart of the Ocean." I was so touched that she gave me something to remind me of the experience we shared. These special moments have left lasting impressions on my heart.

1. Double-underline the **topic sentence**.
2. Underline the **examples** that support the main point.
3. Circle the **transitions**.
4. Does the paragraph have the Four Basics of Good Illustration (p. 73)? Why or why not?
5. Does the paragraph use a particular kind of organization, like time, space, or importance? Does that choice help the paragraph's effectiveness or not?

Professional Illustration Essay

Susan Adams

The Weirdest Job Interview Questions and How to Handle Them

Susan Adams is a senior editor at Forbes, a major publisher of business news. Previously, she was a reporter for the *MacNeil/Lehrer NewsHour*. Adams holds a B.A. from Brown University and a J.D. from Yale University Law School.

Every week, Adams writes an advice column for Forbes.com. In the column reprinted below, she gives examples of some of the stranger questions that come up in job interviews.

1   I once interviewed for a job with a documentary producer who made boring if well-meaning films for public TV. By way of preparation, I studied up on the producer's projects and gave a lot of thought to how my interests and experience dovetailed with his. Our chat went swimmingly until he asked me a question that caught me completely off guard: "Who is your favorite comedian?"

2   Wait a second, I thought. Comedy is the opposite of what this guy does. My mind did back flips while I desperately searched for a comedian who might be a favorite of a tweedy, bearded liberal Democrat. After maybe 30 seconds too long, I blurted out my personal favorite: David Alan Grier, an African-American funnyman on the weekly Fox TV show *In Living Color*. My potential boss looked at me blankly as I babbled about how much I liked Grier's characters, especially Antoine Merriweather, one of the two gay reviewers in the brilliantly hilarious sketch "Men on Film."

3   Wrong answer. I had derailed the interview. My potential employer asked me a few more perfunctory questions and then saw me to the door.

4   We all prepare studiously for job interviews, doing our homework about our potential employers and compiling short but detailed stories to illustrate our accomplishments, but how in the world do we prep for an off-the-wall interview question?

5   Glassdoor.com, a three-year-old Sausalito, California, Web site that bills itself as "the TripAdvisor for careers," has compiled a list of "top oddball interview questions" for two years running. Glassdoor gets its information directly from employees who work at 120,000 companies.

6   Crazy as it sounds, an interviewer at Schlumberger, the giant Houston oilfield services provider, once asked some poor job applicant, "What was your best MacGyver moment?," referring to a 1980s action-adventure TV

show. At Goldman Sachs, the question was, "If you were shrunk to the size of a pencil and put in a blender, how would you get out?" At Deloitte, "How many ridges [are there] around a quarter?" At AT&T, "If you were a superhero, which superhero would you be?" And at Boston Consulting: "How many hair salons are there in Japan?"

No matter where you apply for work, there is a chance you could get a question from left field. According to Rusty Rueff—a consultant at Glassdoor who is the author of *Talent Force: A New Manifesto for the Human Side of Business* and former head of human resources at PepsiCo and Electronic Arts—most job applicants are woefully unprepared for off-the-wall questions. "Ninety percent of people don't know how to deal with them," he says. Like me, they freeze and their minds go blank. 7

To deal with that, Rueff advises, first you have to realize that the interviewer isn't trying to make you look stupid, as stupid as the question may seem. For instance, the MacGyver question is meant as an invitation to talk about how you got out of a tough jam. "They're not looking for you to tell about the time you took out your ballpoint and did a tracheotomy," Rueff notes. Rather, you can probably extract an answer from one of the achievement stories you prepared in advance. 8

With a question like "How many hair salons are there in Japan," the interviewer is giving you an opportunity to demonstrate your thought processes. Rueff says you should think out loud, like the contestants on *Who Wants to Be a Millionaire?* You might start by saying, We'd have to know the population of Japan, and then we'd have to figure out what percentage of them get their hair done and how often. Rueff says it's fine to pull out a pen and paper and start doing some calculations right there in the interview. 9

Connie Thanasoulis-Cerrachio, a career services consultant at Vault .com, agrees with Rueff. "These are called case interview questions," she says. Another example, which may seem equally impossible to answer: Why are manhole covers round? 10

In fact the manhole cover question, and "How would you move Mt. Fuji?," were brought to light in a 2003 book, *How Would You Move Mount Fuji? Microsoft's Cult of the Puzzle: How the World's Smartest Company Selects the Most Creative Thinkers*. Microsoft's grueling interview process often includes such problem-solving and logic questions. Just start thinking through the question, out loud, Thanasoulis-Cerrachio advises. "I would say, a round manhole cover could keep the framework of the tunnel stronger, because a round frame is much stronger than a square frame," she suggests. In fact, there are several reasons, including the fact that a round lid can't fall into the hole the way a square one can and the fact that it can be rolled. 11

Business schools teach students how to deal with case interview questions, and Vault has even put out a book on the subject, *Vault Guide to the Case Interview*. 12

13   Other weird-seeming questions, like "If you were a brick in a wall, which brick would you be and why," or "If you could be any animal, what would you be and why," are really just invitations to show a side of your personality. Thanasoulis-Cerrachio says a friend who is chief executive of a market research company used to ask applicants what kind of car they would be. "She wanted someone fast, who thought quickly," Thanasoulis-Cerrachio says. "She wanted someone who wanted to be a Maserati, not a Bentley." For the brick question, Thanasoulis-Cerrachio advises saying something like, "I would want to be a foundational brick because I'm a solid person. You can build on my experience and I will never let you down."

14   According to Rueff and Thanasoulis-Cerrachio, my comedian question was also a behavioral question, a test of my personality. "You gave a fine answer," says Rueff. Maybe. But I didn't get the job.

Vocabulary development

dovetailed: matched

swimmingly: smoothly; well

perfunctory: quick

studiously: thoroughly; carefully

woefully: seriously; regrettably

tracheotomy: a cut made into the throat to open a blocked airway

grueling: difficult; tiring

Maserati: a fast Italian sports car

Bentley: a British luxury car known more for elegance than speed

1.   In your own words, state Adams's **main point**.

2.   Underline the examples of weird interview questions.

3.   Circle the **transitional words** in paragraph 8. Can you find more places to add transitions?

4.   What do you think of this essay? Do you have a better understanding of how to answer strange questions in job interviews?

Write Your Own Illustration

Write an illustration paragraph, essay, or other document (as described below) on one of the following topics or on one of your own choice. For help, refer to the How to Write Illustration checklist on page 85.

COLLEGE

- Describe your goals for this course, making sure to explain the benefits of achieving each goal.

- Produce a one- or two-page newsletter for other students in your class on one of the following topics. Make sure to describe each club, opportunity, and event in enough detail for readers. Also, include contact information, as well as hours and locations for events and club meetings.

  - Student clubs

  - Volunteer opportunities

  - Upcoming campus events (such as lectures, movies, and sports events)

  - Upcoming events in the larger community

- What is the best or worst job you have ever had? Give examples of what made it the best or worst job.

- Think of the job you would most like to have after graduation. Then, write a list of your skills—both current ones and ones you will be building in college—that are relevant to the job. To identify skills you will be building through your degree program, you might refer to a course catalog. To identify relevant work skills, consider your past or present jobs as well as internships or other work experiences you would like to have before graduation. Finally, write a cover letter explaining why you are the best candidate for your ideal job. Be sure to provide several examples of your skills, referring to the list that you prepared.

- Write about stresses in your life or things that you like about your life. Give plenty of details for each example.

- Give examples of memories that have stayed with you for a long time. Provide enough details so that readers will be able to share your experience.

CHECKLIST: HOW TO WRITE ILLUSTRATION

STEPS	DETAILS
☐ **Narrow and explore your topic.** See Chapter 2.	• Make the topic more specific. • Prewrite to get ideas about the narrowed topic.
☐ **Write a topic sentence (paragraph) or thesis statement (essay).** See Chapter 3.	• State what you want your readers to understand about your topic.
☐ **Support your point.** See Chapter 3.	• Come up with examples and details to show, explain, or prove your main point to readers.
☐ **Write a draft.** See Chapter 4.	• Make a plan that puts examples in a logical order. • Include a topic sentence (paragraph) or thesis statement (essay) and all the supporting examples and details.
☐ **Revise your draft.** See Chapter 4.	• Make sure it has *all* the Four Basics of Good Illustration. • Make sure you include transitions to move readers smoothly from one example to the next.
☐ **Edit your revised draft.** See Chapters 14 through 17.	• Correct errors in grammar, spelling, word use, and punctuation.

7

Description

Writing That Creates Pictures in Words

Understand What Description Is

Description is writing that creates a clear and vivid impression of a person, place, or thing, often by appealing to the physical senses.

Four Basics of Good Description

1. It creates a main impression—an overall effect, feeling, or image—about the topic.

2. It uses specific examples to support the main impression.

3. It supports those examples with details that appeal to the five senses: sight, hearing, smell, taste, and touch.

4. It brings a person, place, or physical object to life for the reader.

In the following student paragraph, the numbers and colors correspond to the Four Basics of Good Description.

Scars are stories written on a person's skin and sometimes on his heart. **1** My scar is not very big or very visible. **2** It is only about three inches long and an inch wide. It is on my knee, so it is usually covered, unseen. **3** It puckers the skin around it, and the texture of the scar itself is smoother than my real skin. It is flesh-colored, almost like a raggedy bandage. The story on my skin is a small one. **1** The story on my heart, though, is much deeper. **2** It was night, very cold, **3** my breath pluming into the frigid air. I took deep breaths that smelled like winter, piercing through my nasal passages and into my lungs as I walked to my car. I saw a couple making out against the wall of a building I was nearing. **2** I smiled and thought about them making their own heat. **3** I thought I saw steam coming from them, but maybe I imagined that. As I got near, I heard a familiar giggle: my girlfriend's. Then I saw her scarlet scarf, one I had given her, along with soft red leather gloves. I turned and ran, before they could see me. There was loud pounding in my ears, from the inside, sounding and feeling as if my brain had just become the loudest bass I had ever heard. My head throbbed, and slipping on some ice, I crashed to the ground, landing on my hands and knees, ripping my pants. I knew my knee was bleeding, even in the dark. I didn't care: **4** That scar would heal. The other one would take a lot longer.

Being able to describe something or someone accurately and in detail is important in many situations.

COLLEGE	On a physical therapy test, you describe the symptoms you observed in a patient.
WORK	You write a memo to your boss describing how the office could be arranged for increased efficiency.
EVERYDAY LIFE	You describe something you lost to the lost-and-found clerk at a store.

In college assignments, the word *describe* may mean *tell about* or *report*. When an assignment asks you to actually describe a person, place, or thing, however, you will need to use the kinds of specific descriptive details discussed later in this chapter.

Main Point in Description

In description, the **main point** is the main impression you want to create for your readers. If you do not have a main impression about your topic, think about how it smells, sounds, looks, tastes, or feels.

PARAGRAPHS VS. ESSAYS IN DESCRIPTION

For more on the important features of description, see the Four Basics of Good Description on page 86.

Paragraph Form

Main Point: Often, narrower for a paragraph than for an essay: While the topic sentence (paragraph) is focused on just one location and view, the thesis statement (essay) sets up descriptions of different views from different sites.

Topic sentence
    The view from the shore of Fisher Lake calms me every time I see it. **Support 1 (first example)** Closest to the shore is the lake's smooth surface, blue by day and sparkling black at night. My favorite time to stand on the shore is midsummer at twilight, when I watch the water's blue darken and become more general, blotting out the day and all its troubles. I listen to waves lapping the dock and think my thoughts, or just let my mind clear. On nights with a bright moon, I stare out at the path of light across the water, losing track of time and sometimes even of myself. **Support 2 (second example)** Farther out, on the opposite shore, a forest of pine trees reminds me of the cool shade I have enjoyed while hiking there. The pine smell is the first thing to trigger the memories. Evenings when there is still enough light, I look for the break in the trees where the main trail starts, thinking of the many times I have walked it. During the hottest, most trying summer of my life, the cool beauty of the trailside trees, ferns, and moss soothed my nerves and brought me back down to earth. **Support 3 (third example)** Beyond the forest are rolling hills, soft gray in the morning and near dusk. The expression "old as the hills" comes to mind, and it feels like a just description, not an insult. The soft gray hulk of them makes me think of an ancient, huge, and eternally sleeping creature—something that predated me by millions of years and will outlive me for millions more. For some reason, I always find these thoughts comforting. **Concluding sentence** And they are just one reason that standing on the shore of Fisher Lake is better for me than any medicine.

Examples Supporting the Main Point (the Writer's Main Impression)

Details about the Examples: Usually, 1 to 3 sentences per example for paragraphs and 3 to 8 sentences per example for essays.

Conclusion

Essay Form

1

I have worked in many places, from a basement-level machine shop to a cubicle in a tenth-floor insurance office. Now that I am in the construction industry, I wan[t to sing the] praises of one employment benef[it that does] not get enough attention: <u>The views from my sky-high welding jobs have been more stunning than any seen through an office window.</u>

Thesis statement

<u>From a platform at my latest job, on a high-rise, the streets below look like scenes from a miniature village.</u> The cars and trucks—even the rushing people—[remind me] of my nephews' motorized toys. [Sometimes] the breeze carries up to me one of the few reminders that what I see is real: the smell of sausage or roasting chestnuts from street vendors, the honking of taxis or the scream of sirens, the dizzying clouds of diesel smoke. Once, the streets below me were taken over

Topic sentence 1 (first example)

2

for a fair, and during my lunch break, I sat on a beam and watched the scene below. I spotted the usual things—packs of people strolling by concession stands or game tents, and bands playing to crowds at different ends of the fair. As I finished my lunch, I saw two small flames near the edge of one band stage, nothing burning, nothing to fear. It was, I soon realized, an acrobat carrying two [torches.] I watched her climb high and walk [a wire,] juggling the torches as the crowd loo[ked up] and I looked down, fascinated.

Topic sentence 2 (second example)

<u>Even more impressive are the sights from an oil rig.</u> Two years ago, I worked on a rig in Prudhoe Bay, Alaska, right at the water's edge. In the long days of summer, I loved to watch the changing light in the sky and on the water: bright to darker blue as the hours passed, and at day's end, a dying gold.

3

At the greatest heights I could see white dots of ships far out at sea, and looking inland, I might spot musk ox or bears roaming in the distance. In the long winter dark, we worked by spotlights, which blotted the views below. But I still remember one time near nightfall when the spotlights suddenly flashed off. As my eyes adjusted, a crowd of carib[ou loomed] below like ghosts. They snuffled t[he frozen] food, oblivious to us.

Topic sentence 3 (third example)

<u>To me, the most amazing views are those from bridges high over rivers.</u> In 2006, I had the privilege of briefly working on one of the tallest bridge-observatories in the world, over the Penobscot River in Maine. As many tourists now do, I reached the height of the observatory's top deck, 437 feet. Unlike them, however, my visits were routine and labor-intensive, giving me little time to appreciate the beauty all around me. But on clear days, during breaks and at the end of our shift,

4

my coworkers and I would admire the wide, sapphire-colored river as it flowed to Penobscot Bay. Looking south, we would track the Maine coast's winding to the Camden Hills. Looking east, we would spot Acadia National Park, the famous Mount Desert Island offshore in the mist. Each sight made up a panoramic [view] that I will never forget.

Concluding paragraph

<u>My line of work roots me in no one place, and it has a generous share of discomforts and dangers. But there are many reasons I would never trade it for another, and one of the biggest is the height from which it lets me see the world. For stretches of time, I feel nearly super human.</u>

The topic sentence (paragraph) or thesis statement (essay) in description usually contains both your narrowed topic and your main impression. Here is a topic sentence for a description paragraph:

The view from the shore of Fisher Lake calms me every time I see it.

Remember that a topic for an essay can be a little broader than one for a paragraph.

The views from my sky-high welding jobs are more stunning than any seen through an office window.

Whereas the topic sentence is focused on just one location and view, the thesis statement sets up descriptions of different views from different sites.

To be effective, your topic sentence or thesis statement should be specific. You can make it specific by adding details that appeal to the senses.

Support in Description

In description, **support** consists of the specific examples and details that help readers experience the sights, sounds, smells, tastes, and textures of your topic. Your description should get your main impression across to readers.

The paragraph and essay models on pages 88–89 use the topic sentence (paragraph) and thesis statement (essay) from the Main Point section of this chapter. Both models include the support used in all descriptive writing—examples that communicate the writer's main impression, backed up by specific sensory details. In the essay model, however, the major support points (examples) are topic sentences for individual paragraphs.

Organization in Description

Description can use any of the orders of organization—**time**, **space**, or **importance**—depending on your purpose. (For more on these orders of organization, see pages 42–43.)If you are writing to create a main impression of an event (for example, a description of fireworks), you might use time order. If you are describing what someone or something looks like, you might use space order, the strategy used in the paragraph model on page 88. If one detail about your topic is stronger than the others, you could use order of importance and leave that detail for last. This approach is taken in the essay model on page 89.

Use **transitions** to move your readers from one sensory detail to the next. Usually, transitions should match your order of organization. For a list of transition words, see pages 56–57.

Read and Analyze Description

After you read each of the selections below, answer the questions that follow.

Description in the Real World

Celia Hyde, Chief of Police

Report, Breaking and Entering Scene
Response to Burglar Alarm, 17:00 Hours

After attending college, Celia Hyde entered the field of law enforcement. She is currently the chief of police in the town of Bolton, Massachusetts. In her job, Celia's writing includes policies, reports, budgets, and statements from victims and criminals. In all her writing, Hyde needs to choose her words carefully to avoid any confusion and misunderstanding. Below is one example of the descriptive reports Celia writes every day.

The house at 123 Main Street is situated off the road with a long, narrow driveway and no visible neighbors. The dense fir trees along the drive block natural light, though it was almost dusk and getting dark. There was snow on the driveway from a recent storm. I observed one set of fresh tire marks entering the driveway and a set of footprints exiting it.

The homeowner, Mr. Smith, had been awakened by the sounds of smashing glass and the squeaking of the door as it opened. He felt a cold draft from the stairway and heard a soft shuffle of feet crossing the dining room. Smith descended the stairs to investigate and was met at the bottom by the intruder, who shoved him against the wall and ran out the front door.

While awaiting backup, I obtained a description of the intruder from Mr. Smith. The subject was a white male, approximately 25–30 years of age and 5′9″–5′11″ in height. He had jet-black hair of medium length, and it was worn slicked back from his forehead. He wore a salt-and-pepper, closely shaved beard and had a birthmark on his neck the size of a dime. The subject was wearing a black nylon jacket with some logo on it in large white letters, a blue plaid shirt, and blue jeans.

1.   What is your **main impression** of the scene and of the intruder?
2.   Underline the **details** that support the main impression.
3.   What senses do the details appeal to?
4.   How is the description organized?

Student Description Paragraph

Alessandra Cepeda

Bird Rescue

Alessandra Cepeda became deeply involved in animal welfare during her time at Bunker Hill Community College (BHCC), from which she received associate's degrees in education and early childhood education. While at BHCC, Cepeda assisted the Humane Society with animal-rescue efforts.

In the following paragraph, Cepeda describes the scene at a storage unit containing abandoned birds. One of those birds was Samantha, shown in the photo with Cepeda.

When the owner opened the empty storage unit, we could not believe that any living creature could have survived under such horrible conditions. The inside was complete darkness, with no windows and no ventilation. The air hit us with the smell of rot and decay. A flashlight revealed three birds, quiet and huddled in the back corner. They were quivering and looked sickly. Two of the birds had injured wings, hanging from them uselessly at odd angles, obviously broken. They were exotic birds who should have had bright and colorful feathers, but the floor of the unit was covered in the feathers they had molted. We entered slowly and retrieved the abused birds. I cried at how such beautiful and helpless creatures had been mistreated. We adopted two of them, and our Samantha is now eight years old, with beautiful green feathers topped off with a brilliant blue and red head. She talks, flies, and is a wonderful pet who is dearly loved and, I admit, very spoiled. She deserves it after such a rough start to her life.

1. Double-underline the **topic sentence**.

2. What main impression does the writer create?

3. Underline the **sensory details** (sight, sound, smell, taste, texture) that create the main impression.

4. Does the paragraph have the Four Basics of Good Description (p. 86)? Why or why not?

Professional Description Essay

Oscar Hijuelos

Memories of New York City Snow

Oscar Hijuelos, the son of Cuban immigrants, was born in New York City in 1951. After receiving undergraduate and master's degrees from the City University of New York, he took a job at an advertising firm and wrote fiction at night. His first novel, *The Mambo Kings Play Songs of Love* (1989), was awarded the Pulitzer Prize for fiction, making Hijuelos the first Hispanic writer to receive this honor. His most recent novels include *Dark Dude* (2008) and *Beautiful Maria of My Soul* (2010).

The following essay was taken from the anthology *Metropolis Found* (2003). In it, Hijuelos describes a New York City winter from the perspective of new immigrants.

1   For immigrants of my parents' generation, who had first come to New York City from the much warmer climate of Cuba in the mid-1940s, the very existence of snow was a source of fascination. A black-and-white photograph that I have always loved, circa 1948, its surface cracked like that of a thawing ice-covered pond, features my father, Pascual, and my godfather,

[1] Oriente
Province:
a former
province of
Cuba, in the
eastern part
of the country

Horacio, fresh up from **Oriente Province**,[1] posing in a snow-covered meadow in Central Park. Decked out in long coats, scarves, and black-rimmed hats, they are holding, in their be-gloved hands, a huge chunk of hardened snow. Trees and their straggly witch's hair branches, glimmering with ice and frost, recede into the distance behind them. They stand on a field of whiteness, the two men seemingly afloat in midair, as if they were being held aloft by the magical substance itself.

That they bothered to have this photograph taken—I suppose to send   2
back to family in Cuba—has always been a source of enchantment for me. That something so common to winters in New York would strike them as an object of exotic admiration has always spoken volumes about the new-ness—and innocence—of their immigrants' experience. How thrilling it all must have seemed to them, for their New York was so very different from the small town surrounded by farms in eastern Cuba that they hailed from. Their New York was a fanciful and bustling city of endless sidewalks and unimaginably high buildings; of great bridges and twisting outdoor elevated train trestles; of walkup tenement houses with mysteriously dark base-ments, and subways that burrowed through an underworld of girded tun-nels; of dancehalls, burlesque houses, and palatial department stores with their complement of Christmas Salvation Army Santa Clauses on every street corner. Delightful and perilous, their New York was a city of incred-ibly loud noises, of police and air raid sirens and factory whistles and sub-way rumble; a city where people sometimes shushed you for speaking Spanish in a public place, or could be unforgiving if you did not speak English well or seemed to be of a different ethnic background. (My father was once nearly hit by a garbage can that had been thrown off the rooftop of a building as he was walking along La Salle Street in upper Manhattan.)

Even so, New York represented the future. The city meant jobs and   3
money. Newly arrived, an aunt of mine went to work for Pan Am; another aunt, as a Macy's saleslady. My own mother, speaking nary a word of Eng-lish, did a stint in the garment district as a seamstress. During the war some family friends, like my godfather, were eventually drafted, while others ended up as factory laborers. Landing a job at the Biltmore Men's Bar, my father joined the hotel and restaurant workers' union, paid his first weekly dues, and came home one day with a brand new white chef's toque in hand. Just about everybody found work, often for low pay and ridiculously long hours. And while the men of that generation worked a lot of overtime, or a second job, they always had their day or two off. Dressed to the hilt, they'd leave their uptown neighborhoods and make an excursion to another part of the city—perhaps to one of the grand movie palaces of Times Square or to beautiful Central Park, as my father and godfather, and their ladies, had once done, in the aftermath of a snowfall.

Snow, such as it can only fall in New York City, was not just about the   4
cold and wintry differences that mark the weather of the north. It was about a purity that would descend upon the grayness of its streets like a heaven of

silence, the city's complexity and bustle abruptly subdued. But as beautiful as it could be, it was also something that provoked nostalgia; I am certain that my father would miss Cuba on some bitterly cold days. I remember that whenever we were out on a walk and it began to snow, my father would stop and look up at the sky, with wonderment—what he was seeing I don't know. Perhaps that's why to this day my own associations with a New York City snowfall have a mystical connotation, as if the presence of snow really meant that some kind of inaccessible divinity had settled his breath upon us.

1. Double-underline the **thesis statement**.
2. Underline the **sensory details** (sight, sound, smell, taste, texture).
3. Circle the **transitions**.
4. Does the essay create a clear picture of New York City in the winter? Why or why not?

Write Your Own Description

Write a description paragraph or essay on one of the following topics or on one of your own choice. For help, refer to the How to Write Description checklist on page 96.

COLLEGE

■ Describe the sights, sounds, smells, and tastes in the cafeteria or another dining spot on campus.

■ Find a place where you can get a good view of your campus (for instance, a window on an upper floor of one of the buildings). Then, describe the scene using space order (pp. 42–43).

WORK

■ Describe your workplace, including as many sensory details as you can.

■ Describe your boss or a colleague you work with closely. First, think of the main impression you get from this person. Then, choose details that would make your impression clear to readers.

EVERYDAY LIFE

■ Describe a holiday celebration from your past, including as many sensory details as possible. Think back on the people who attended, the food served, the decorations, and so on.

■ Visit an organization that serves your community, such as an animal shelter or a food pantry. During your visit, take notes about what you see. Later, write a detailed description of the scene.

Vocabulary development

circa: [taken] around

aloft: high

trestles: support structures

tenement houses: apartment buildings, often crowded and in poor shape

girded: reinforced

burlesque houses: theaters that offer live, often humorous performances and/ or striptease acts

palatial: palace-like

perilous: dangerous

nary: not even

stint: brief job

toque: hat

to the hilt: [dressed] in the fanciest clothing

nostalgia: a longing for something from the past

connotation: meaning or association

inaccessible divinity: unreachable god

CHECKLIST: HOW TO WRITE DESCRIPTION	
STEPS	**DETAILS**
☐ **Narrow and explore your topic.** See Chapter 2.	• Make the topic more specific. • Prewrite to get ideas about the narrowed topic.
☐ **Write a topic sentence (paragraph) or thesis statement (essay).** See Chapter 3.	• State what is most interesting, vivid, and important about your topic.
☐ **Support your point.** See Chapter 3.	• Come up with examples and details that create a main impression about your topic.
☐ **Write a draft.** See Chapter 4.	• Make a plan that puts examples in a logical order. • Include a topic sentence (paragraph) or thesis statement (essay) and all the supporting examples and details.
☐ **Revise your draft.** See Chapter 4.	• Make sure it has *all* the Four Basics of Good Description. • Make sure you include transitions to move readers smoothly from one detail to the next.
☐ **Edit your revised draft.** See Chapters 14 through 17.	• Correct errors in grammar, spelling, word use, and punctuation.

8

Process Analysis

Writing That Explains How Things Happen

Understand What Process Analysis Is

Process analysis either explains how to do something (so that your readers can do it) or explains how something works (so that your readers can understand it).

Four Basics of Good Process Analysis

1. It tells readers what process the writer wants them to know about and makes a point about it.
2. It presents the essential steps in the process.
3. It explains the steps in detail.
4. It presents the steps in a logical order (usually time order).

In the following paragraph, the numbers and colors correspond to the Four Basics of Good Process Analysis.

The poet Dana Gioia once said, "Art delights, instructs, con- **4** soles. It educates our emotions." **1** Closely observing paintings, Time sculpture, and other forms of visual art is a great way to have the type of experience that Gioia describes, and following a few basic steps will help you get the most from the experience. **2** First, choose an art exhibit that interests you. **3** You can find listings

LearningCurve For extra practice in the skills covered in this chapter, visit: bedfordstmartins.com/rwinteractive.

97

for exhibits on local museums' Web sites or in the arts section of a newspaper. Links on the Web sites or articles in a newspaper may give you more information about the exhibits, the artists featured in them, and the types of work to be displayed. **2** Second, go to the museum with an open mind and, ideally, with a friend. **3** While moving through the exhibit, take time to examine each work carefully. As you do so, ask yourself questions: What is my eye most drawn to, and why? What questions does this work raise for me, and how does it make me feel? How would I describe it to someone over the phone? Ask your friend the same questions, and consider the responses. You might also consult an exhibit brochure for information about the featured artists and their works. **2** Finally, keep your exploration going after you have left the museum. **3** Go out for coffee or a meal with your friend. Trade more of your thoughts and ideas about the artwork, and discuss your overall impressions. If you are especially interested in any of the artists or their works, you might look for additional information or images on the Internet, or you might consult books at the library. Throughout the whole experience, put aside the common belief that only artists or cultural experts "get" art. The artist Eugène Delacroix described paintings as "a bridge between the soul of the artist and that of the spectator." Trust your ability to cross that bridge and come to new understandings.

You use process analysis in many situations:

COLLEGE	In a science course, you explain photosynthesis.
WORK	You write instructions to explain how to operate something (the copier, the fax machine).
EVERYDAY LIFE	You write out a recipe for an aunt.

In college, a writing assignment may ask you to *describe the process of,* but you might be asked to *describe the stages of* _____ or *explain how* _____ *works*. Whenever you need to identify and explain the steps or stages of anything, you will use process analysis.

Main Point in Process Analysis

In process analysis, your **purpose** is to explain how to do something or how something works. Your **main point** should tell readers what process you are describing and what you want readers to know about it. Here is an example of a topic sentence for a paragraph:

Sealing windows against the cold is an easy way to reduce heating bills.

Remember that the topic for an essay can be a little broader than one for a paragraph.

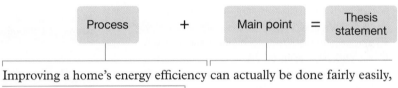

Improving a home's energy efficiency can actually be done fairly easily, significantly lowering utility bills.

Whereas the topic sentence focuses on just one method to improve energy efficiency, the thesis statement sets up a discussion of multiple methods.

Support in Process Analysis

The paragraph and essay models on pages 100–101 use the topic sentence (paragraph) and thesis statement (essay) from the Main Point section of this chapter. Both models include the **support** used in all writing about processes: the steps in the process backed up by details about these steps. In the essay model, however, the major support points (steps) are topic sentences for individual paragraphs.

Organization in Process Analysis

Process analysis is usually organized by **time order** because it explains the steps of the process in the order in which they occur, starting with the first step. (For more on time order, see page 42.) This is the strategy used in the paragraph and essay models on pages 100–101.

PARAGRAPHS VS. ESSAYS IN PROCESS ANALYSIS

For more on the important features of process analysis, see the Four Basics of Good Process Analysis on page 97.

Paragraph Form

Main Point: Often, narrower for a paragraph than for an essay: While the topic sentence (paragraph) focuses on just one method to improve energy efficiency, the thesis statement (essay) sets up a discussion of multiple methods.

Topic sentence

Sealing windows against the cold is an easy way to reduce heating bills. **Support 1 (first step)** First, make sure the inside window frames are clean and clear of dust. Often, it is enough to wipe the frames with a soft, dry cloth. However, if the frames are especially dirty, clean them thoroughly with a damp cloth, and then dry them with paper towels or a blow dryer. **Support 2 (second step)** Next, apply two-sided adhesive tape on all four sides of the window frame. Begin by peeling the cover from one side of the adhesive. Then, affix this side of the tape to the frame. After you have taped all four sides of the frame, remove the front side of the adhesive cover. **Support 3 (third step)** Finally, attach the plastic sheeting to the tape. Start by measuring your window and cutting the plastic so that it fits. Next, apply the plastic to the tape, starting at the top of the window and working your way down. When the plastic is fully attached, seal it over the window by running a blow dryer over the plastic from top to bottom. **Concluding sentence** By spending one morning or afternoon covering your windows, you can save $300 on your heating bills and enjoy a much more comfortable home.

Support for the Main Point (the Steps of a Process)

Details about the Steps: Usually, 1 to 3 sentences per step for paragraphs and 3 to 8 sentences per step for essays.

Conclusion

Essay Form

1

Many people are intimidated by the work necessary to make their home energy efficient, and they do not see ~~**Thesis statement**~~ it-yourself job. However, improving a home's energy efficiency can actually be done fairly easily, significantly lowering utility bills.

Thesis statement

First, seal air leaks around windows and doors. To seal air leaks around wind caulk between window frames and if you have old-fashioned windows t weather-proof, cover them with plastic before the cold temperatures set in. This process involves affixing two-sided adhesive tape to the window frames and then attaching plastic sheeting, which is sealed with the use of a blow dryer. Next, look for drafty spots around doors. Many air leaks at the top or sides of doors can be sealed with adhesive-backed foam strips. Leaks under doors can be stopped with foam

Topic sentence 1 (first step)

2

draft guards. Alternatively, a rolled-up blanket, rug, or towel can keep the cold from coming in. All of these measures can save up to $600 per season on heating bills.

Second, install water-saving shower heads and faucet aerators. These fixt inexpensive and are available in most h stores. Also, they are easy to instal. unscrew the old shower or faucet head. Then, follow the package instructions for affixing the new shower head or aerator. In some cases, you might have to use pipe tape or a rubber washer to ensure a good seal. After this step, run the water to make sure there are no leaks. If you find any leaks, use pliers to tighten the seal. In time, you will discover that the new shower heads and aerators will cut your water usage and the cost of water heating by up to 50 percent.

Topic sentence 2 (second step)

3

Finally, look for other places where energy efficiency could be increased. One simple improvement is to re traditional light bulbs with compact fluorescent which use up to 80 percent less energy. Also, make your insulation is as good as it can be. Many utilities now offer free assessments of home insulation, identifying places where it is missing or inadequate. In some cases, any necessary insulation improvements may be subsidized by the utilities or by government agencies. It is well worth considering such improvements, which, in the case of poorly insulated homes, can save thousands of dollars a year, quickly covering any costs. Although some people prefer to have professionals blow insulating foam into their walls, it is not difficult to add insulation to attics, where a large amount of heat can be lost during cold months.

Topic sentence 3 (third step)

Taking even one of these steps can make a significant financial difference in your life and also reduce your impact on the environment. My advice, though, is to improve home's energy efficiency as much as possible, ever means doing just a little at a time. The long-term payoff is too big to pass up.

Concluding paragraph

Transitions move readers smoothly from one step to the next.

Common Transitions in Process Analysis

after	eventually	meanwhile	since
as	finally	next	soon
at last	first	now	then
before	last	once	when
during	later	second	while

Read and Analyze Process Analysis

After you read each of the selections below, answer the questions that follow.

Process Analysis in the Real World

Jeremy Graham, Youth Pastor and Motivational Speaker

Becoming a Community Leader

Jeremy Graham grew up in a nice home in New Orleans, but when he was thirteen and his father moved out, Jeremy's life took a turn for the worse. Faced with stress and financial difficulty, Jeremy dropped out of school and began selling drugs. Fortunately, Jeremy's mother and his pastor encouraged him to attend community college, where he earned a degree in business administration and accounting. Jeremy is now the youth pastor at his church, and he is working toward his bachelor's degree at Mississippi College. The paragraph below is an example of the instructional material Jeremy writes for his job.

As a member of a youth group, you can become an active leader in the group and in your larger community. Following a few key steps can help you along the way. The first step is to lead by example. Older group members must set the path for younger members by showing them how to conduct themselves, work hard, and keep a positive attitude in any situation.

By doing so, the younger members will build healthy relationships, and the skills they learn from older mentors will help them in school and future jobs. Second, youth leaders must encourage their peers to get involved with the community to make positive changes. Gathering together young people to visit homeless shelters, feed the homeless, and clean up the community are just a few things that can be done. These activities teach youth to be grateful for their living conditions and to extend a helping hand to others. The third step is to build good character and moral integrity. This happens naturally as youth leaders become more involved in their communities and serve as role models for other youth. Having good character and integrity improves young leaders' lives and helps them continue to have a positive impact on others. To sum up, all these steps greatly benefit youth leaders and the communities they serve.

1.   What **process** is being analyzed?
2.   How many steps does Jeremy give?
3.   In your own words, what are the steps to becoming an effective leader?

Student Process Analysis Paragraph

Charlton Brown

Buying a Car at an Auction

Buying a car at an auction is a good way to get a cheap car, but buyers need to be prepared. First, decide what kind of vehicle you want to buy. Then, find a local auction. Scams are common, though, so be careful. Three top sites that are legitimate are www.gov-auctions.org, www.carauctioninc.com, and www.seizecars.com. When you have found an auction and a vehicle you are interested in, become a savvy buyer. Make sure you know the car's actual market value. You can find this out from Edmunds.com, Kellybluebook.com, or NADA (the National Automobile Dealers Association). Because bidding can become like a competition, decide on the highest bid you will make, and stick to that. Do not get drawn into the competition. On the day of the auction, get to the auction early so that you can look at the actual cars. If you do not know about cars yourself, bring someone who does with you to the auction so that he or she can examine the car. Next, begin your thorough examination. Check the exterior; especially look for any signs that the car has been in an accident. Also, check the windshield because many states will not give an inspection sticker to cars with any damage to the windshield. Check the interior and try the brakes. Start the engine and listen to how it sounds. Check the heat and air conditioning, the CD player, and all other functions. As a final check before the bidding, look at the car's engine and transmission. Finally, get ready to place your bid, and remember, do not go beyond the amount you settled on earlier. Good luck!

Vocabulary development

legitimate: lawful; genuine; real

savvy: knowledgeable; well informed

bid: an offer, in this case, of a price

thorough: complete; detailed

1.   Double-underline the **topic sentence**.

2.   What is Charlton's **main point**?

3.   Underline the **major steps**.

4.   Circle the transition words that signal when Charlton moves from one step to the next.

5.   Does Charlton's paragraph follow the Four Basics of Good Process Analysis (p. 97)? Why or why not?

Professional Process Analysis Essay

Ian Frazier

How to Operate the Shower Curtain

Born in 1951 in Cleveland, Ohio, writer Ian Frazier is known both for his humorous essays and for his more serious explorations of subjects ranging from American history to fishing. A staff writer for the *New Yorker,* Frazier has contributed pieces to the magazine since 1974, shortly after his graduation from Harvard University. He has also published several books, most recently *Lamentations of the Father* (2008), and *Travels in Siberia* (2010).

In the following process analysis essay, Frazier finds humor in one source of annoyance for many people.

Dear Guest: The shower curtain in this bathroom has been purchased 1 with care at a reputable "big box" store in order to provide maximum convenience in showering. After you have read these instructions, you will find with a little practice that our shower curtain is as easy to use as the one you have at home.

You'll note that the shower curtain consists of several parts. The top 2 hem, closest to the ceiling, contains a series of regularly spaced holes designed for the insertion of shower-curtain rings. As this part receives much of the everyday strain of usage, it must be handled correctly. Grasp the shower curtain by its leading edge and gently pull until it is flush with the wall. Step into the tub, if you have not already done so. Then take the other edge of shower curtain and cautiously pull it in opposite direction until it, too, adjoins the wall.

3   Keep in mind that normal bathing will cause you unavoidably to bump against shower curtain, which may cling to you for a moment owing to the natural adhesiveness of water. Some guests find the sensation of wet plastic on their naked flesh upsetting, and overreact to it. Instead, pinch the shower curtain between your thumb and forefinger near where it is adhering to you and simply move away from it until it is disengaged. Then, with the ends of your fingers, push it back to where it is supposed to be.

4   Many guests are surprised to learn that all water pipes in our system run off a single riser. This means that the opening of any hot or cold tap, or the flushing of a toilet, interrupts flow to shower. If you find water becoming extremely hot (or cold), exit tub promptly while using a sweeping motion with one arm to push shower curtain aside.

5   REMEMBER TO KEEP SHOWER CURTAIN INSIDE TUB AT ALL TIMES! Failure to do this may result in baseboard rot, wallpaper mildew, destruction of living-room ceiling below, and possible dripping onto catered refreshments at social event in your honor that you are about to attend. So be careful!

6   When detaching shower curtain from clinging to you or when exiting tub during a change in water temperature, bear in mind that there are seventeen mostly empty plastic bottles of shampoo on tub edge next to wall. These bottles have accumulated in this area over time. Many have been set upside down in order to concentrate the last amounts of fluid in their cap mechanisms, and are balanced lightly. Inadvertent contact with a thigh or knee can cause all the bottles to be knocked over and to tumble into the tub or behind it.

7   While picking up the bottles, a guest occasionally will lose his or her balance temporarily, and, in even rarer cases, fall. If you find this occurring, remember that panic is the enemy here. Let your body go limp, while reminding yourself that the shower curtain is not designed to bear your weight. Grabbing onto it will only complicate the situation.

8   If, in a "worst case" scenario, you do take hold of the shower curtain, and the curtain rings tear through the holes in the upper hem as you were warned they might, remain motionless and relaxed in the position in which you come to rest. If subsequently you hear a knock on the bathroom door, respond to any questions by saying either "Fine" or "No, I'm fine." When the questioner goes away, stand up, turn off shower, and lay shower curtain flat on floor and up against tub so you can see the extent of the damage. With a sharp object — a nail file, a pen, or your teeth — make new holes in top hem next to the ones that tore through.

9   Now lift shower curtain with both hands and reattach it to shower-curtain rings by unclipping, inserting, and reclipping them. If during this process the shower curtain slides down and again goes onto you, reach behind you to shelf

under medicine cabinet, take nail file or curved fingernail scissors, and perform short, brisk slashing jabs on shower curtain to cut it back. It can always
be repaired later with safety pins or adhesive tape from your toiletries kit.

At this point, you may prefer to get the shower curtain out of your way   10
entirely by gathering it up with both arms and ripping it down with a sharp
yank. Now place it in the waste receptacle next to the john. In order that
anyone who might be overhearing you will know that you are still all right,
sing "Fat Bottomed Girls," by Queen,[1] as loudly as necessary. While waiting
for tub to fill, wedge shower curtain into waste receptacle more firmly by
treading it underfoot with a regular high-knee action as if marching in place.

[1] **Queen:**
British rock
band popular
in the 1970s
and 1980s

**Vocabulary
development**

reputable:
having a good
reputation

owing to: as a
result of

disengaged:
removed

riser: vertical
pipe

detaching:
removing

inadvertent:
unintentional;
accidental

scenario:
situation

subsequently:
afterward

receptacle:
container

john: slang for
toilet

1. The first paragraph contains what seems to be the **thesis statement**.
    Double-underline it.

2. Circle the **transitions** that introduce steps in the process.

3. Does this essay follow the Four Basics of Good Process Analysis
    (p. 97)? Why or why not?

Write Your Own Process Analysis

Write a process analysis paragraph or essay on one of the following topics
or on one of your own choice. For help, refer to the How to Write Process
Analysis checklist on page 107.

COLLEGE

■ Describe the process of preparing for an exam.

■ Attend a tutoring session at your college's writing center. Afterward,
   describe the process: What specific things did the tutor do to help you?
   Also, explain what you learned from the process.

WORK

■ Describe how to make a positive impression at a job interview.

■ Think of a challenging task you had to accomplish at work. What steps
   did you go through to complete it?

EVERYDAY LIFE

■ Describe the process of making something, such as a favorite meal, a
   set of shelves, or a sweater.

■ Take part in a community activity, such as a fund-raising event for a
   charity, a neighborhood cleanup, or food preparation at a homeless
   shelter. Then, describe the process you went through.

CHECKLIST: HOW TO WRITE PROCESS ANALYSIS

STEPS	DETAILS
☐ **Narrow and explore your topic.** See Chapter 2.	• Make the topic more specific. • Prewrite to get ideas about the narrowed topic.
☐ **Write a topic sentence (paragraph) or thesis statement (essay).** See Chapter 3.	• Decide what you want readers to know about the process you are describing.
☐ **Support your point.** See Chapter 3.	• Include the steps in the process, and explain the steps in detail.
☐ **Write a draft.** See Chapter 4.	• Make a plan that puts examples in a logical order. • Include a topic sentence (paragraph) or thesis statement (essay) and all the supporting details about each step.
☐ **Revise your draft.** See Chapter 4.	• Make sure it has *all* the Four Basics of Good Process Analysis. • Make sure you include transitions to move readers smoothly from one step to the next.
☐ **Edit your revised draft.** See Chapters 14 through 17.	• Correct errors in grammar, spelling, word use, and punctuation.

9

Classification

Writing That Sorts Things into Groups

Understand What Classification Is

Classification is writing that organizes, or sorts, people or items into categories. It uses an **organizing principle**: *how* the people or items are sorted. The organizing principle is directly related to the purpose for classifying. For example, you might sort clean laundry (your purpose) using one of the following organizing principles: by ownership (yours, your roommate's) or by where it goes (the bedroom, the bathroom).

Four Basics of Good Classification

1 It makes sense of a group of people or items by organizing them into categories.

2 It has a purpose for sorting the people or items.

3 It categorizes using a single organizing principle.

4 It gives detailed explanations or examples of what fits into each category.

In the following paragraph, the numbers and colors correspond to the Four Basics of Good Classification.

1 In researching careers I might pursue, I have learned that there are three major types of workers, **2** each having different strengths and preferences. **3** The first type of worker is a big-picture person, who likes to look toward the future and think of new businesses, products, and services. **4** Big-picture people

✓ **LearningCurve** For extra practice in the skills covered in this chapter, visit: bedfordstmartins.com/rwinteractive.

might also identify ways to make their workplaces more successful and productive. Often, they hold leadership positions, achieving their goals by assigning specific projects and tasks to others. Big-picture people may be drawn to starting their own businesses. Or they might manage or become a consultant for an existing business. **3** The second type of worker is a detail person, who focuses on the smaller picture, whether it be a floor plan in a construction project, a spreadsheet showing a business's revenue and expenses, or data from a scientific experiment. **4** Detail people take pride in understanding all the ins and outs of a task and doing everything carefully and well. Some detail people prefer to work with their hands, doing such things as carpentry or electrical wiring. Others prefer office jobs, such as accounting or clerical work. Detail people may also be drawn to technical careers, such as scientific research or engineering. **3** The third type of worker is a people person, who gets a lot of satisfaction from reaching out to others and helping meet their needs. **4** A people person has good social skills and likes to get out in the world to use them. Therefore, this type of worker is unlikely to be happy sitting behind a desk. A successful people person often shares qualities of the other types of workers; for example, he or she may show leadership potential. In addition, his or her job may require careful attention to detail. Good jobs for a people person include teaching, sales, nursing, and other health-care positions. Having evaluated my own strengths and preferences, I believe that I am equal parts big-picture person and people person. I am happy to see that I have many career options.

You use classification anytime you want to organize people or items.

COLLEGE	In a criminal justice course, you are asked to discuss the most common types of chronic offenders.
WORK	For a sales presentation, you classify the kinds of products your company produces.
EVERYDAY LIFE	You classify your typical monthly expenses to make a budget.

In college, writing assignments probably will not use the word *classification*. Instead, you might be asked to *describe the types of* _____ or *explain the types or kinds of* _____. You might also be asked, *How is* _____ *organized?* or *What are the parts of* _____? Words and phrases that signal that you need to sort things into categories require classification.

Main Point in Classification

The **main point** in classification uses a single **organizing principle** to sort items in a way that serves your purpose. The categories should help you achieve your purpose. The main point may or may not state the organizing principle directly. Look at the following examples:

TOPIC SENTENCE:

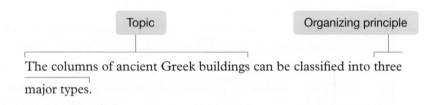

The columns of ancient Greek buildings can be classified into three major types.

THESIS STATEMENT:

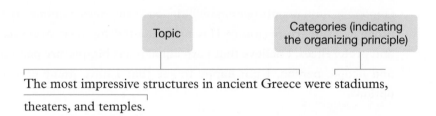

The most impressive structures in ancient Greece were stadiums, theaters, and temples.

In both main points, the organizing principle is *types* of things — columns in the case of the paragraph and buildings in the case of the essay. The thesis statement does not state this principle directly, however. Instead, the categories — stadiums, theaters, and temples — make the principle clear.

Also, notice that the topic for the essay is broader than the one for the paragraph, which is often the case.

Support in Classification

The paragraph and essay models on pages 112–13 use the topic sentence (paragraph) and thesis statement (essay) from the Main Point section of this chapter. Both models include the **support** used in all classification writing: categories backed up by explanations or examples of each category. In the essay model, however, the major support points (categories) are topic sentences for individual paragraphs.

Organization in Classification

Classification can be organized in different ways (**time order**, **space order**, or **order of importance**) depending on its purpose. (For more on the orders of organization, see pages 42–43.)

PURPOSE	LIKELY ORGANIZATION
to explain changes or events over time	time
to describe the arrangement of people/ items in physical space	space
to discuss parts of an issue or problem, or types of people or things	importance

Order of importance is used in the essay model on page 113.

As you write your classification, use **transitions** to move your readers smoothly from one category to another.

Common Transitions in Classification

another	for example
another kind	for instance
first, second, third, and so on	last
	one example/another example

PARAGRAPHS VS. ESSAYS IN CLASSIFICATION

For more on the important features of classification, see the Four Basics of Good Classification on page 108.

Paragraph Form

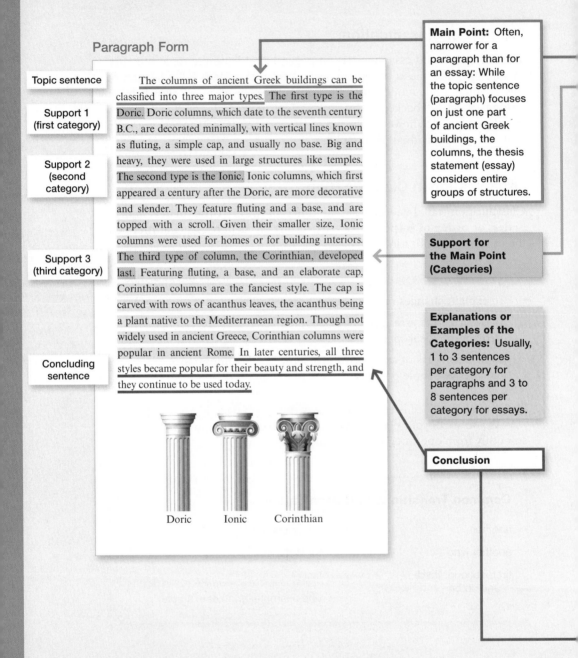

Topic sentence

   The columns of ancient Greek buildings can be classified into three major types. The first type is the Doric.

Support 1 (first category)

Doric columns, which date to the seventh century B.C., are decorated minimally, with vertical lines known as fluting, a simple cap, and usually no base. Big and heavy, they were used in large structures like temples.

Support 2 (second category)

The second type is the Ionic. Ionic columns, which first appeared a century after the Doric, are more decorative and slender. They feature fluting and a base, and are topped with a scroll. Given their smaller size, Ionic columns were used for homes or for building interiors.

Support 3 (third category)

The third type of column, the Corinthian, developed last. Featuring fluting, a base, and an elaborate cap, Corinthian columns are the fanciest style. The cap is carved with rows of acanthus leaves, the acanthus being a plant native to the Mediterranean region. Though not widely used in ancient Greece, Corinthian columns were popular in ancient Rome.

Concluding sentence

In later centuries, all three styles became popular for their beauty and strength, and they continue to be used today.

Doric   Ionic   Corinthian

Main Point: Often, narrower for a paragraph than for an essay: While the topic sentence (paragraph) focuses on just one part of ancient Greek buildings, the columns, the thesis statement (essay) considers entire groups of structures.

Support for the Main Point (Categories)

Explanations or Examples of the Categories: Usually, 1 to 3 sentences per category for paragraphs and 3 to 8 sentences per category for essays.

Conclusion

Essay Form

Ancient Greek civilization **Thesis statement** wealth of architectural wonders th beautiful and lasting. The most impressive structures were stadiums, theaters, and temples.

The stadiums were designed to hold thousands of spectators. These op **Topic sentence 1 (first category)** were set into hillsides so that the s stone benches, would rise up fron. space, giving all spectators a decent view. One of the most famous stadiums, built in Delphi in the fifth century B.C., seated audiences of about 7,000 people. Many stadiums featured ornamental details such as dramatic arches, and some of the more sophisticated examples included heated bathhouses with heated floors. Most often, the stadiums hosted sp **Topic sentence 2 (second category)** such as foot races. A common racing the "stade," equaling one length of

Another type of structure, the theater, was also a popular public gathering place. Like stadiums, the theaters were open-air sites that

were set into hillsides. But instead of sports, they featured plays, musical performances, poetry readings, and other cultural events. In the typical Greek theater, a central performance area was surrounded by semicircular seating, which was often broken into different sections. Wooden, and later stone, stages were set up in the central area, and in front of the stage was a space used for singing and dancing. This space was known as the "orchestra." Among the most famous ancient Greek theaters is the one at Epidaurus built in the fourth century B.C. and s **Topic sentence 3 (third category)** 14,000 people. Performances still take

The most beautiful structures were the temples, with their grand entrances and large open spaces. Temples were rectangular in shape, and their outer walls as well as some interior spaces were supported by columns. Their main structures were typically made of limestone or marble, while their roofs might be constructed of terra-cotta or marble tiles. Temples were

created to serve as "homes" for particular gods or goddesses, who were represented by statues. People left food or other offerings to these gods or goddesses to stay in their good graces, and communities often held festivals and other celebrations in their honor. Temples tended to be built in either the Doric or Ionic style, with Doric temples featuring simple, heavy columns and Ionic temples featuring slightly more ornate columns. The most famous temple, in the Doric style, is the Parthenon in Athens.

Concluding paragraph Turning to the present day, many modern stadiums, theaters, and columned civic buildings show the influence of ancient Greek buildings. Recognizing the lasting strength and beauty of these old structures, architects and designers continue to return to them for inspiration. I predict that this inspiration will last at least a thousand more years.

Read and Analyze Classification

After you read each of the selections below, answer the questions that folllow.

Classification in the Real World

Leigh King, Fashion Writer / Blogger

Prom Fashions

When she was a student at the Fashion Institute of Design & Merchandising (FIDM), Leigh King used the skills she learned in her introduction-to-writing course to start a fashion blog. Blogging helped Leigh get noticed in the competitive world of New York City fashion, where she got an internship at *Teen Vogue* magazine. Leigh is now a self-employed fashion writer and blogger. Below is part of an e-mail that Leigh sent to colleagues about upcoming blog posts.

Now that we're on the eve of prom season, I am going to be writing about some of the most eye-catching prom fashions:

- **Dresses:** The newest looks range from classic and romantic, to glittery and modern, to vintage. And the new styles come in a variety of colors, from understated cream, to striking black and white, to candy colors or pastels.

- **Clutch purses:** There are plenty of new looks to choose from, including purses made of bold-patterned fabrics or accented with stylish beading.

- **Shoes:** No matter what style of dress a prom-goer chooses, there are beautiful shoes to go with it: ballet flats, chunky wooden heels, heels with jewels or bows, and more.

1. Double-underline the **main point** of the e-mail.

2. What categories does Leigh break the fashions into?

3. Does the e-mail have the Four Basics of Good Classification (p. 108)?

Student Classification Paragraph

Lorenza Mattazi

All My Music

    From the time I was young, I have always loved music, all kinds of music. My first experience of music was the opera that both of my parents always had playing in our house. I learned to understand the drama and emotion of operas. My parents both spoke Italian, and they told me the stories of the operas and translated the words sung in Italian to English so that I could understand. Because hearing opera made my parents happy, and they taught me about it, I loved it, too. Many of my friends think I am weird when I say I love opera, but to me it is very emotional and beautiful. When I was in my early teens, I found rock music and listened to it no matter what I was doing. I like the music with words that tell a story that I can relate to. In that way, rock can be like opera, with stories that everyone can relate to, about love, heartbreak, happiness, and pain. The best rock has powerful guitars and bass, and a good, strong drumbeat. I love it when I can feel the bass in my chest. Rock has good energy and power. Now, I love rap music, too, not the rap with words that are violent or disrespectful of women, but the rest. The words are poetry, and the energy is so high that I feel as if I just have to move my body to the beat. That rhythm is so steady. I have even written some good rap, which my friends say is really good. Maybe I will try to get it published, even on something like Helium, or I could start a blog. I will always love music because it is a good way to communicate feelings and stories, and it makes people feel good.

1. Double-underline the **topic sentence**.
2. What **categories** of music does Lorenza write about?
3. Circle the **transitions**.
4. Does the paragraph have the Four Basics of Good Classification (p. 108)? Why or why not?
5. What kind of organization does Lorenza use?

Professional Classification Essay

Frances Cole Jones

Don't Work in a Goat's Stomach

Frances Cole Jones, who holds a B.A. in English/creative writing from Connecticut College and an M.A. in liberal studies from New York University, is founder and president of Cole Media Management, a firm that focuses on improving clients' communication skills. Jones has also published her own books: *How to Wow: Proven Strategies for Presenting Your Ideas, Persuading Your Audience, and Perfecting Your Image* (2008) and *The Wow Factor: The 33 Things You Must (and Must Not) Do to Guarantee Your Edge in Today's Business World* (2010).

In the following excerpt from *The Wow Factor,* Jones discusses the types of workplace clutter that can get in the way of success on the job.

When I was working in the nine-to-five world, there was a gentleman 1 down the hall whose office inevitably looked like it had been stirred up with a stick: a desk loaded with piles of paper, dirty cups, takeout containers, a Magic 8 Ball,[1] and a keyboard that looked like you'd be better off wearing a hazmat suit when you touched it, more piles of papers on the desk, on the floor, on the chairs; shelving that was loaded with books, photos, and (bizarrely) pieces of sporting equipment, various items of clothing tossed hither and yon: jackets, sweaters, socks, shoes, hats. . . . One day, our boss walked by and said, "That office looks like the inside of a goat's stomach."

Not surprisingly, the occupant of the messy office wasn't with the com- 2 pany much longer.

What I've learned since then is that my colleague had created a petri dish 3 of the three kinds of recognized office clutter. As identified by psychologist Sam Gosling, they are "identity clutter": photos of family, friends, pets, etc. that are designed to remind us we have a life outside the office; "thought and feeling regulators," which are chosen to change our mood: squeezable stress balls, miniature Zen gardens,[2] daily affirmation calendars;[3] and "behavior residues"—old coffee cups, food wrappers, Post-its stuck to the keyboard, etc.

The trouble with having a disproportionate number of these items in 4 and around your office is that it sends a message to those around you that you are out of control. As one of my CEO clients said to me after we'd walked past his junior report's disastrously messy office on the way to his company's conference room, "Doesn't she realize I notice—and care?"

Now I'm not saying you can't have a few personal items. And I am cer- 5 tainly not going to mandate, as one of my clients has done, what kinds of

[1] **Magic 8 Ball:** a fortune-telling toy that when shaken provides answers to questions

[2] **Zen gardens:** miniature (in this case) gardens meant to create a peaceful setting

[3] **affirmation calendars:** calendars that include encouraging sayings

flowers you are allowed to receive. In that office, your loved ones can send you a white orchid. That's it. But I am saying it's important to choose carefully, cull frequently, and clean daily.

6   In an effort to help you decide what stays and what goes, I have put together two lists: Remove Immediately and Keep Selectively. Given its urgency, let's first look at those items I'd prefer you remove immediately.

Remove Immediately:

- Leftover food: food wrappers; dirty cups, plates, or silverware. While this may seem self-evident, I imagine that more than a few of you have found yourself at five o'clock speaking to your coworkers from amid a small forest of half-empty coffee cups. (And I am hoping there are at least one or two of you who—like me—are still drinking absentmindedly from your 8 a.m. coffee at 5 p.m., a practice I'm prone to if not carefully supervised, which always makes my assistant exclaim with disgust.) All of these must go—again, if you're like me, for your own sake if no one else's. When you do remove them, please don't simply dump them in the sink of the shared kitchen down the hall. I know of one office that based its recent decision as to which of two equally qualified and experienced people was laid off on who was more prone to leaving their dirty dishes in the communal kitchen; deciding factors these days are, indeed, this small.

- Dead flowers/plants. The roses your ex gave you last Valentine's Day shouldn't become a dried flower arrangement on the shelf. That shedding ficus tree will be much happier if given to a friend with a green thumb.

- Stuffed animals/"whimsical" toys (such as the aforementioned Magic 8 Ball). While these can be helpful should your—or your boss's—kids come to the office, day to day they have the potential to undermine others' perceptions of the professionalism you bring to your work.

Keep Selectively:

- Grooming products. Hairbrushes, toothbrushes/paste, shaving and nail paraphernalia can all be handy to have on hand. Please don't, however, leave them in plain sight—or perform any personal maintenance in front of others.

- Extra pairs of shoes/a shirt. Again, both are useful on days when you have an unexpectedly important meeting, or uncooperative weather. They should, however, be stowed out of others' sight lines.

- Photos of family/friends. While these are lovely reminders of your life outside the office and can be great conversation starters, please do make sure everyone in each photo is fully clothed and behaving appropriately. . . .

All this said, I do know that an office has to be worked in—and that 7 worrying about keeping it pristine can, ultimately, detract from focusing on what you need to accomplish. For this reason, it can help to set aside fifteen minutes at the middle and end of each day to clear your desk/chairs/floor of any accumulated clutter. A principle applied by airlines and luxury bus lines, these intermittent sweeps help keep things from piling up.

1.   Double-underline the **thesis statement**.

2.   Within the categories "Remove Immediately" and "Keep Selectively," Jones presents six subcategories of things. Underline them.

3.   Circle the **transitions.**

4.   Do you agree with Jones's categorizations? For instance, do you see value in keeping any of the things Jones thinks should be removed immediately? Why or why not?

Write Your Own Classification

Write a classification paragraph or essay on one of the following topics or on one of your own choice. For help, refer to the How to Write Classification checklist on page 119.

COLLEGE

■   Classify the types of resources available in your college's library, giving examples of things in each category. If you don't have time to visit the library, spend time looking at its Web site. (Some library Web sites include virtual tours.)

■   Classify the course requirements for your program into different categories, such as easy, challenging, and very challenging. Your purpose could be to help a future student in the program understand what to expect.

WORK

■   Classify the different types of bosses, giving explanations and examples for each category.

■   Classify the types of skills you need in your current job or a job you held in the past. Give explanations and examples for each category of skill.

EVERYDAY LIFE

■ Using Lorenza Mattazi's paragraph as a guide (see p. 115), classify the types of music you enjoy.

■ Write about the types of challenges you face in your everyday life, giving explanations and examples for each category.

CHECKLIST: HOW TO WRITE CLASSIFICATION

STEPS	DETAILS
☐ Narrow and explore your topic. See Chapter 2.	• Make the topic more specific. • Prewrite to get ideas about the narrowed topic.
☐ Write a topic sentence (paragraph) or thesis statement (essay). See Chapter 3.	• State your topic and your organizing principle or categories.
☐ Support your point. See Chapter 3.	• Come up with explanations/examples to support each category.
☐ Write a draft. See Chapter 4.	• Make a plan that puts the categories in a logical order. • Include a topic sentence (paragraph) or thesis statement (essay) and all the supporting categories with explanations and examples.
☐ Revise your draft. See Chapter 4.	• Make sure it has *all* the Four Basics of Good Classification. • Make sure you include transitions to move readers smoothly from one category to the next.
☐ Edit your revised draft. See Chapters 14 through 17.	• Correct errors in grammar, spelling, word use, and punctuation.

10

Definition

Writing That Tells What Something Means

Understand What Definition Is

Definition is writing that explains what a term or concept means.

Four Basics of Good Definition

1 It tells readers what is being defined.

2 It presents a clear definition.

3 It uses examples to show what the writer means.

4 It gives details to support the examples.

In the following paragraph, the numbers and colors correspond to the Four Basics of Good Definition.

A **1** stereotype **2** is a conventional idea or image that is simplistic—and often wrong, particularly when it is applied to people or groups of people. Stereotypes can prevent us from seeing people as they really are because stereotypes blind us with preconceived notions about what a certain type of person is like. **3** For example, I had a stereotyped notion of Native Americans until I met my friend Daniel, a Chippewa Indian. **4** I thought all Indians wore feathers and beads, had long black hair, and avoided all

LearningCurve For extra practice in the skills covered in this chapter, visit: bedfordstmartins.com/rwinteractive.

contact with non–Native Americans because they resented their land being taken away. Daniel, however, wears jeans and T-shirts, and we talk about everything—even our different ancestries. After meeting him, I understood that my stereotype of Native Americans was completely wrong. **3** Not only was it wrong, but it set up an us-them concept in my mind that made me feel that I, as a non–Native American, would never have anything in common with Native Americans. My stereotype would not have allowed me to see any Native American as an individual: I would have seen him or her as part of a group that I thought was all alike, and all different from me. From now on, I won't assume that any individual fits my stereotype; I will try to see that person as I would like them to see me: as myself, not a stereotyped image.

You can use definition in many practical situations.

COLLEGE	On a math exam, you are asked to define *exponential notation*.
WORK	On a job application, you are asked to choose one word that describes you and explain why.
EVERYDAY LIFE	In a relationship, you define for your partner what you mean by *commitment* or *communication*.

In college, writing assignments may include the word *define*, but they might also use phrases such as *explain the meaning of* _____ and *discuss the meaning of* _____. In these cases, use the strategies discussed in this chapter to complete the assignment.

Main Point in Definition

In definition, the **main point** usually defines a term or concept. The main point is related to your purpose: to help your readers understand the term or concept as you are using it.

When you write your definition, do not just copy the dictionary definition; write it in your own words as you want your readers to understand it. Your topic sentence (paragraph) or thesis statement (essay) can take the following forms.

PARAGRAPHS VS. ESSAYS IN DEFINITION

For more on the important features of definition, see the Four Basics of Good Definition on page 120.

Paragraph Form

Topic sentence

Support 1 (first example)

Support 2 (second example)

Support 3 (third example)

Concluding sentence

Phototherapy means treating seasonal depression through exposure to light. One form of phototherapy is spending time outdoors during the brightest time of day. Noon until 2 p.m. is ideal, but going outside earlier or later is better than not getting out at all. Because the sun sets earlier in the winter, it might be necessary to step outdoors before the end of a workday, perhaps during a lunch break. Alternatively, face a bright window for twenty to thirty minutes and absorb the rays. Another form of phototherapy is the use of a lamp that mimics outdoor light. Typically, people sit by these lamps as they read, work, or watch television. It is best to use them for at least twenty minutes a day. Apart from sunlight, the most effective form of phototherapy is the use of a light-therapy box. Some experts believe that light boxes allow users to absorb more light than is possible with the lamps, which tend to be smaller. However, both phototherapy lamps and light boxes are good ways to counter winter darkness and cloudy days in any season. Whether the solution is a lamp, a light box, or good old-fashioned sunlight, there is no reason to suffer from seasonal depression.

Main Point: Often, narrower for a paragraph than for an essay: While the topic sentence (paragraph) focuses on just one treatment for seasonal affective disorder, the thesis statement (essay) considers the disorder as a whole.

Examples Supporting the Main Point

Details about the Examples: Usually, 1 to 3 sentences per example for paragraphs and 3 to 8 sentences per example for essays.

Conclusion

Essay

1

Seasonal affective disorder (SAD) is a form of depression caused by inadequate exposure to sunlight in fall or winter. It can seriously affect the daily life of ~~suffer from it.~~ **Thesis statement**

One consequence of SAD is sleepiness and a lack of energy. SAD suffer **Topic sentence 1 (first example)** that they are sleeping longer yet ar during the day, especially during th Connected to the drowsiness may be moodiness and an inability to concentrate. The latter effect can result in poorer performance at work and at other tasks. Those affected by SAD may also find that they move more slowly than usual and that all types of physical activity are more challenging than they u **Topic sentence 2 (second example)** these difficulties can be a source o sometimes worsening the depressi

Another consequence of SAD is loss of interest in work, hobbies, and other activities.

2

To some extent, these symptoms may be connected to a lack of energy. Often, however, the feelings run deeper than that. Activities that once lifted one's spirits may have the opposite effect. For instance, a mother who at one time never missed her child's soccer games might now see attending them as a burden. Someone who was once a top performer at work may find that it is all he or she can do to show **Topic sentence 3 (third example)** morning. Such changes in one's out contribute to a feeling of hopelessness

The most serious consequence of SAD is withdrawal from interactions with others. SAD sufferers may find that they are no longer interested in going out with friends, and they may turn down requests to get together for movies, meals, or social events. They may even withdraw from family members, engaging less frequently in conversation or even spending time alone in their rooms. Furthermore,

3

they may postpone or cancel activities, such as vacation trips, that might require them to interact with family for hours at a time. Withdrawal symptoms may also extend to the workplace, with SAD sufferers becoming less vocal at meetings or avoiding lunches or conversations with colleagues. Concern that family members or coworkers may be noticing such personality changes can cause or worsen anxiety in those with SAD.

Concluding paragraph

Because the effects of SAD can be so significant, it is important to address them as soon as possible. Fortunately, there are many good therapies for the condition, from drug treatment to greater exposure to sunlight, whether real or simulated through special lamps or light boxes. Often, such treatments have SAD sufferers feeling better quickly.

TOPIC SENTENCE:

Phototherapy is a treatment for depression caused by inadequate exposure to sunlight.

In this example, "Class" is the larger group the term belongs to. Main-point statements do not have to include a class, however. For example:

TOPIC SENTENCE:

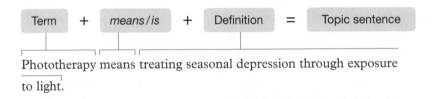

Phototherapy means treating seasonal depression through exposure to light.

Now, look at this thesis statement about a related topic.

THESIS STATEMENT:

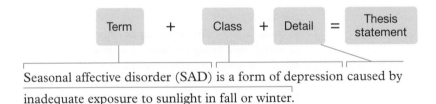

Seasonal affective disorder (SAD) is a form of depression caused by inadequate exposure to sunlight in fall or winter.

The thesis statement is broader in scope than the topic sentences, because it sets up a discussion of the larger subject of seasonal affective disorder. In contrast, the topic sentences consider one particular treatment for this disorder (phototherapy).

Support in Definition

The paragraph and essay models on pages 122–23 use one topic sentence (paragraph) and the thesis statement (essay) from the Main Point section in this chapter. Both models include the **support** used in all definition writing: examples that explain what a term or concept means backed up by details about these examples. In the essay model, however, the major support points (examples) are topic sentences for individual paragraphs.

Organization in Definition

The examples in definition are often organized by **order of importance**, meaning that the example that will have the most effect on readers is saved for last. (For more on order of importance, see page 43.) This strategy is used in the paragraph and essay models on pages 122–23.

Transitions in definition move readers from one example to the next. Here are some transitions you might use in definition, although many others are possible, too.

Common Transitions in Definition

another; one/another   for example

another kind   for instance

first, second, third, and so on

Read and Analyze Definition

After you read each of the selections below, answer the questions that follow.

Definition in the Real World

Walter Scanlon, Program and Workplace Consultant
Employee Assistance Program

Walter Scanlon got hooked early on drugs and alcohol and spent a decade on the streets and in and out of hospitals and prisons. He turned his life around after joining Alcoholics Anonymous and earned a GED, a B.A. from Pace University, an M.B.A. from New York Institute of Technology, and finally a Ph.D. from Columbus University. As the owner of a successful consulting business, Walter does all kinds of writing: letters, proposals, presentations, e-mails, and memos. He has also published two books and numerous professional articles. In the paragraph below, Walter defines "employee assistance program" for a client.

The "employee assistance program" (EAP) is a confidential, early-intervention workplace counseling service designed to help employees who are experiencing personal problems. It is a social service within a work environment that can be found in most major corporations, associations, and government organizations. EAP services are always free to the employee and benefit the organization as much as the employee. Employees who are free of emotional problems are far more productive than those who are not. An employee whose productivity is negatively affected by a drinking problem, for example, might seek help through the EAP. He/she would be assessed by a counselor and then referred to an appropriate community resource for additional services. The *employee* is helped through the EAP while the *employer* is rewarded with improved productivity. An EAP is a win-win program for all involved.

1.   Double-underline the **topic sentence**.
2.   Identify the term defined in the paragraph and define it in your own words.
3.   Underline an **example** of what an EAP might do.
4.   Double-underline the sentence that makes a final observation about the topic.

Student Definition Paragraph

Corin Costas

What Community Involvement Means to Me

While at Bunker Hill Community College (BHCC), Corin Costas helped start a business club on campus. Later, he took on the leadership of SHOCWAVES (Students Helping Our Community with Activities), where Costas initiated several projects, including Light One Little Candle, which raised money for the Dana-Farber Cancer Institute to buy books for children with cancer. After graduating from BHCC, Costas transferred to the University of Massachusetts Boston with a $14,000 scholarship.

In the following paragraph, Costas defines SHOCWAVES and what it does.

SHOCWAVES is a student organization at Bunker Hill Community College. SHOCWAVES stands for Students Helping Our Community with Activities, and its mission is to get students involved with the community— to become part of it by actively working in it in positive ways. Each year, SHOCWAVES is assigned a budget by the Student Activities Office, and it spends that budget in activities that help the community in a variety of ways. Some of the money is spent, for example, in fund-raising events for community causes. We have money to plan and launch a fund-raiser, which raises far more than we spend. In the process, other students and members of the community also become involved in the helping effort. We get to know lots of people, and we usually have a lot of fun—all while helping others. Recently, we have worked as part of the Charles River Cleanup, the Walk for Hunger, collecting toys for sick and needy children, and Light One Little Candle. While SHOCWAVES's mission is to help the community, it also benefits its members. Working in the community, I have learned so many valuable skills, and I always have something I care about to write about for my classes. I have learned about budgeting, advertising, organizing, and managing. I have also developed my creativity by coming up with new ways to do things. I have networked with many people, including people who are important in the business world. SHOCWAVES has greatly improved my life, and my chances for future success.

1. Double-underline the **topic sentence**.

2. Underline the **examples** of what SHOCWAVES does for the community.

3. Double-underline the sentence that makes a final observation about the topic.

4. Does this paragraph follow the Four Basics of Good Definition (p. 120)? Why or why not?

Professional Definition Essay

Janice E. Castro with Dan Cook and Cristina Garcia

Spanglish

Janice E. Castro is an assistant professor in the Medill New Media Program at Northwestern University. She worked as a reporter for *Time* for more than twenty years and started the magazine's health policy beat. After the publication of her book, *The American Way of Health* (1994), she became the managing editor of *Time*'s online division.

Castro wrote "Spanglish" while at *Time* with the help of Dan Cook and Cristina Garcia. In the essay, she defines the language created when Spanish and English speakers come together.

In Manhattan a first-grader greets her visiting grandparents, happily 1
exclaiming, "Come here, *siéntate!*" Her bemused grandfather, who does not
speak Spanish, nevertheless knows she is asking him to sit down. A Miami
personnel officer understands what a job applicant means when he says,
"*Quiero un* part time." Nor do drivers miss a beat reading a billboard along-
side a Los Angeles street advertising CERVEZA—SIX-PACK!

This free-form blend of Spanish and English, known as Spanglish, is 2
common linguistic currency wherever concentrations of Hispanic Americans are found in the U.S. In Los Angeles, where 55 percent of the city's 3
million inhabitants speak Spanish, Spanglish is as much a part of daily life
as sunglasses. Unlike the broken-English efforts of earlier immigrants from
Europe, Asia, and other regions, Spanglish has become a widely accepted
conversational mode used casually—even playfully—by Spanish-speaking
immigrants and native-born Americans alike.

Consisting of one part Hispanicized English, one part Americanized 3
Spanish, and more than a little fractured syntax, Spanglish is a bit like a
Robin Williams comedy routine: a crackling line of cross-cultural patter
straight from the melting pot. Often it enters Anglo homes and families
through the children, who pick it up at school or at play with their young
Hispanic contemporaries. In other cases, it comes from watching TV; many
an Anglo child watching *Sesame Street* has learned *uno dos tres* almost as
quickly as one two three.

Spanglish takes a variety of forms, from the Southern California 4
Anglos who bid farewell with the utterly silly "*hasta la* bye-bye" to the
Cuban American drivers in Miami who *parquean* their *carros.* Some Spanglish sentences are mostly Spanish, with a quick detour for an English
word or two. A Latino friend may cut short a conversation by glancing at
his watch and excusing himself with the explanation that he must "*ir al*
supermarket.*"

Many of the English words transplanted in this way are simply hardier 5
than their Spanish counterparts. No matter how distasteful the subject, for
example, it is still easier to say "income tax" than *impuesto sobre la renta.* At
the same time, many Spanish-speaking immigrants have adopted such terms
as *VCR, microwave,* and *dishwasher* for what they view as largely American
phenomena. Still other English words convey a cultural context that is not
implicit in the Spanish. A friend who invites you to *lonche* most likely has in
mind the brisk American custom of "doing lunch" rather than the languorous afternoon break traditionally implied by *almuerzo.*

Mainstream Americans exposed to similar hybrids of German, Chi- 6
nese, or Hindi might be mystified. But even Anglos who speak little or no
Spanish are somewhat familiar with Spanglish. Living among them, for

one thing, are 19 million Hispanics. In addition, more American high school and university students sign up for Spanish than for any other foreign language.

7   Only in the past ten years [in 1978–1988], though, has Spanglish begun to turn into a national slang. Its popularity has grown with the explosive increases in U.S. immigration from Latin American countries. English has increasingly collided with Spanish in retail stores, offices and classrooms, in pop music, and on street corners. Anglos whose ancestors picked up such Spanish words as *rancho, bronco, tornado,* and *incommunicado,* for instance, now freely use such Spanish words as *gracias, bueno, amigo,* and *por favor.*

8   Among Latinos, Spanglish conversations often flow easily from Spanish into several sentences of English and back.

9   Spanglish is a sort of code for Latinos: the speakers know Spanish, but their hybrid language reflects the American culture in which they live. Many lean to shorter, clipped phrases in place of the longer, more graceful expressions their parents used. Says Leonel de la Cuesta, an assistant professor of modern languages at Florida International University in Miami: "In the U.S., time is money, and that is showing up in Spanglish as an economy of language." Conversational examples: *taipiar* (type) and *winshiwiper* (windshield wiper) replace *escribir a máquina* and *limpiaparabrisas.*

10   Major advertisers, eager to tap the estimated $134 billion in spending power wielded by Spanish-speaking Americans, have ventured into Spanglish to promote their products. In some cases, attempts to sprinkle Spanish through commercials have produced embarrassing gaffes. A Braniff Airlines ad that sought to tell Spanish-speaking audiences they could settle back *en* (in) luxuriant *cuero* (leather) seats, for example, inadvertently said they could fly without clothes (*encuero*). A fractured translation of the Miller Lite slogan told readers the beer was "Filling, and less delicious." Similar blunders are often made by Anglos trying to impress Spanish-speaking pals. But if Latinos are amused by mangled Spanglish, they also recognize these goofs as a sort of friendly acceptance. As they might put it, *no problema.*

1.   Double-underline the **thesis statement**.

2.   Circle the **transitions** used to introduce examples.

3.   Do the writers provide enough examples of what they mean by *Spanglish*? If not, where could more examples be added?

4.   Look back at the final paragraph. Why do you suppose the authors chose to conclude in that way?

Vocabulary development

bemused: surprised and a bit confused

linguistic currency: typical speech

fractured syntax: language that breaks grammatical rules

patter: quick speech

melting pot: a blending of people from different cultures

Anglo: a white, English-speaking person

contemporaries: peers

phenomena: strange experiences or things

implicit: understood but not expressed directly

languorous: long and relaxing

hybrid: a combination of two things

wielded: held

gaffes: mistakes

inadvertently: by mistake; not intentionally

blunders: mistakes

Write Your Own Definition

Write a definition paragraph or essay on one of the following topics or on one of your own choice. For help, refer to the How to Write Definition checklist on page 131.

COLLEGE

- How would you define a good student or a bad student? Give examples to explain your definition.

- Identify a difficult or technical term from a class you are taking. Then, define the term, and give examples of different ways in which it might be used.

WORK

- Define a satisfying job, giving explanations and examples.

- If you have ever held a job that used unusual or interesting terminology, write about some of the terms used, what they meant, and their function on the job.

EVERYDAY LIFE

- What does it mean to be a good friend? Provide a definition, giving explanations and examples.

- What does it mean to be a good parent? Provide a definition, giving explanations and examples.

CHECKLIST: HOW TO WRITE DEFINITION

STEPS	DETAILS
☐ **Narrow and explore your topic.** See Chapter 2.	• Make the topic more specific. • Prewrite to get ideas about the narrowed topic.
☐ **Write a topic sentence (paragraph) or thesis statement (essay).** See Chapter 3.	• State the term that you are focusing on, and provide a definition for it.
☐ **Support your point.** See Chapter 3.	• Come up with examples and details to explain your definition.
☐ **Write a draft.** See Chapter 4.	• Make a plan that puts the examples in a logical order. • Include a topic sentence (paragraph) or thesis statement (essay) and all the supporting examples and details.
☐ **Revise your draft.** See Chapter 4.	• Make sure it has *all* the Four Basics of Good Definition. • Make sure you include transitions to move readers smoothly from one example to the next.
☐ **Edit your revised draft.** See Chapters 14 through 17.	• Correct errors in grammar, spelling, word use, and punctuation.

Comparison and Contrast

*Writing That Shows Similarities
and Differences*

Understand What Comparison and Contrast Are

Comparison is writing that shows the similarities among subjects—people, ideas, situations, or items; **contrast** shows the differences. In conversation, people often use the word *compare* to mean either compare or contrast, but as you work through this chapter, the terms will be separated.

| Compare | = | Similarities |

| Contrast | = | Differences |

Four Basics of Good Comparison and Contrast

1. It uses subjects that have enough in common to be compared/contrasted in a useful way.
2. It serves a purpose—to help readers make a decision, to help them understand the subjects, or to show your understanding of the subjects.
3. It presents several important, parallel points of comparison/contrast.
4. It arranges points in a logical order.

In the following paragraph, written for a biology course, the numbers and colors correspond to the Four Basics of Good Comparison and Contrast.

✓ LearningCurve For extra practice in the skills covered in this chapter, visit:
bedfordstmartins.com/rwinteractive.

1 Although frogs and toads are closely related, **2** they differ in appearance, in habitat, and in behavior. **3** The first major difference is in the creatures' physical characteristics. Whereas most frogs have smooth, slimy skin that helps them move through water, toads tend to have rough, bumpy skin suited to drier surroundings. Also, whereas frogs have long, muscular hind legs that help them leap away from predators or toward food, most toads have shorter legs and, therefore, less ability to move quickly. Another physical characteristic of frogs and toads is their bulging eyes, which help them see in different directions. This ability is important, because neither creature can turn its head to look for food or spot a predator. However, frogs' eyes may protrude more than toads'. The second major difference between frogs and toads is their choice of habitat. Frogs tend to live in or near ponds, lakes, or other sources of water. In contrast, toads live mostly in drier areas, such as gardens, forests, and fields. But, like frogs, they lay their eggs in water. The third major difference between frogs and toads concerns their behavior. Whereas frogs may be active during the day or at night, most toads keep a low profile until nighttime. Some biologists believe that it is nature's way of making up for toads' inability to escape from danger as quickly as frogs can. At night, toads are less likely to be spotted by predators. Finally, although both frogs and toads tend to live by themselves, toads, unlike frogs, may form groups while they are hibernating. Both creatures can teach us a lot about how animals adapt to their environments, and studying them is a lot of fun.

4 Points arranged in a logical order

Many situations require you to understand similarities and differences.

COLLEGE	In a pharmacy course, you compare and contrast the side effects of two drugs prescribed for the same illness.
WORK	You are asked to contrast this year's sales with last year's.
EVERYDAY LIFE	At the supermarket, you contrast brands of the same food to decide which to buy.

In college, writing assignments may include the words *compare and contrast,* but they might also use phrases such as *discuss similarities and differences, how is* X *like (or unlike)* Y?, or *what do* X *and* Y *have in common?* Also, assignments may use only the word *compare.*

Main Point in Comparison and Contrast

The **main point** should state the subjects you want to compare or contrast and help you achieve your purpose. Your topic sentence (paragraph) or thesis statement (essay) identifies the subjects and states the main point you want to make about them. Here is an example of a topic sentence for a paragraph:

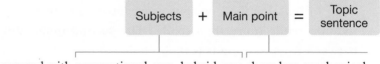

Compared with conventional cars, hybrid cars show less mechanical wear over time.

Remember that the topic for an essay can be a little broader than one for a paragraph.

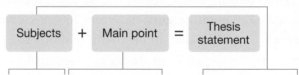

A hybrid car is a better choice than a conventional car, even one with low gas mileage.

Whereas the topic sentence focuses on the mechanical advantages of hybrid cars, the thesis statement sets up a broader discussion of these cars' benefits.

Support in Comparison and Contrast

The paragraph and essay models on pages 136–37 use the topic sentence (paragraph) and thesis statement (essay) from the Main Point section in this chapter. Both models include the **support** used in all comparison and contrast writing: points of comparison/contrast backed up by details. In the essay model, however, the points of comparison/contrast are topic sentences for individual paragraphs.

The support in comparison/contrast should show how your subjects are the same or different. To find support, many people make a list with two columns, one for each subject, with parallel points of comparison or contrast.

TOPIC SENTENCE/THESIS STATEMENT: The two credit cards I am considering offer different financial terms.

BIG CARD	MEGA CARD
no annual fee	$35 annual fee
$1 fee per cash advance	$1.50 fee per cash advance
30 days before interest charges begin	25 days before interest charges begin
15.5% finance charge	17.9% finance charge

Choose points that will be convincing and understandable to your readers. Explain your points with facts, details, or examples.

Organization in Comparison and Contrast

Comparison/contrast can be organized in one of two ways: A **point-by-point** organization presents one point of comparison or contrast between the subjects and then moves to the next point. (See the essay model on page 137.) A **whole-to-whole** organization presents all the points of comparison or contrast for one subject and then all the points for the next subject. (See the paragraph model on page 136.) Consider which organization will best explain the similarities or differences to your readers. Whichever organization you choose, stay with it throughout your writing.

Comparison/contrast is often organized by **order of importance**, meaning that the most important point is saved for last. (For more on order of importance, see page 43.) This strategy is used in the essay model on page 137.

Transitions in comparison/contrast move readers from one subject to another and from one point of comparison or contrast to the next.

Common Transitions in Comparison and Contrast

COMPARISON	CONTRAST
both	in contrast
like/unlike	most important difference
most important similarity	now/then
one similarity/another similarity	one difference/another difference
similarly	unlike
	while

PARAGRAPHS VS. ESSAYS IN COMPARISON AND CONTRAST

For more on the important features of comparison and contrast, see the Four Basics of Good Comparison and Contrast on page 132.

Paragraph Form

Topic sentence	Compared with conventional cars, hybrid cars show less mechanical wear over time. In conventional vehicles,
Support 1 (first point of comparison/contrast)	braking and idling place continual stress on the engine and brakes. When braking, drivers of such vehicles rely completely on the friction of the brake pads to come to a stop. As a result, brakes wear down over time, sometimes rather quickly. Additionally, these vehicles burn gas
Support 2 (second point of comparison/contrast)	even while idling, making the engine use unnecessary energy and fuel. In contrast, hybrid cars are designed to reduce brake and engine wear. Say that a hybrid driver is moving from a sixty-mile-per-hour stretch of highway to a twenty-five-mile-per-hour off-ramp. When he or she brakes, the hybrid's motor goes into reverse, slowing the car and allowing the driver to place less strain on the brakes. Then, as the driver enters stop-and-start traffic in town, the electric motor takes over from the gas engine, improving energy efficiency during idling and reducing engine wear.
Concluding sentence	These mechanical benefits of hybrids can lead to lower maintenance costs, a significant improvement over conventional cars.

Main Point: Often, narrower for a paragraph than for an essay: While the topic sentence (paragraph) focuses on the mechanical advantages of hybrid cars, the thesis statement (essay) sets up a broader discussion of these cars' benefits.

Support for the Main Point (Points of Comparison/Contrast)

Details about Each Point of Comparison/Contrast: Usually, 1 to 3 sentences per point for paragraphs and 3 to 8 sentences per point for essays.

Conclusion

Essay Form

They are too expensive. For the last two years, while trying to keep my dying 1999 Chevy on the road, these words have popped into my head every time I have thought about ~~buying~~ a hybrid car. But now that I have ~~done my~~ research, I am finally convinced: A hybrid car is a better choice than a conventional car, even one with low gas mileage.

> **Thesis statement**

The first advantage of hybrid cars over conventional cars is that buyers can get tax breaks and other hybrid-specific benefits. Although federal tax credits for hybrid purch~~ases ended~~ in 2010, several states, including ~~Colorado,~~ Louisiana, Maryland, and New Mex~~ico continue~~ to offer such credits. Also, in Ariz~~ona~~ and several other states, hybrid drivers are allowed to use the less congested high-occupancy vehicle (HOV) lanes even if the driver is the only person on board. Additional benefits for hybrid drivers include longer warranties than those offered for

> **Topic sentence 1 (first point of comparison/ contrast)**

conventional cars and, in some states and cities, rebates, reduced licensing fees, and free parking. None of these benefits are offered to drivers of conventional cars.

The second advantage of hybrid cars over conventional cars is that they save money over the long term. In addition to using ~~less gas,~~ hybrids show less mechanical wear a~~nd tear,~~ reducing maintenance costs. When ~~braking,~~ drivers of conventional cars rely c~~ompletely~~ on the friction of the brake pads to come to a stop. As a result, brakes wear down over time, sometimes rather quickly. Additionally, these vehicles burn gas even while idling, making the engine use unnecessary energy and fuel. In contrast, when hybrid drivers hit the brakes, the car's motor goes into reverse, slowing the car and allowing the driver to place less strain on the brakes. Then, as the driver enters stop-and-start traffic in town, the electric motor takes over from

> **Topic sentence 2 (second point of comparison/ contrast)**

the gas engine, improving energy efficiency during idling and reducing engine wear.

The most important benefit of hybrid cars over conventional cars is that they have a lower impact on the environment. Experts estimate that each gallon of gas burned by con~~ventional~~ motor vehicles produces 28 pounds of carbon dioxide ~~, a~~ greenhouse gas that is a major contributor to global ~~warming.~~ Because hybrid cars use about half as much gas as con~~ventional~~ vehicles, they reduce pollution and greenhouse gases by at least 50 percent. Some experts estimate that they reduce such emissions by as much as 80 percent. The National Resources Defense Council says that if hybrid vehicles are widely adopted, annual reductions in emissions could reach 450 million metric tons by the year 2050. This reduction would be equal to taking 82.5 million cars off the road.

> **Topic sentence 3 (third point of comparison/ contrast)**

Although hybrid cars are more expensive than conventional cars, they are well worth it. From an economic standpoint, they save on fuel and maintenance costs. But, to me, the best reasons for buying a hybrid are ethical: By switching to such a vehicle, I will help reduce my toll on the environment. So goodbye, 1999 Chevy, and hello, Toyota Prius!

> **Concluding paragraph**

Read and Analyze Comparison and Contrast

After you read each of the selections below, answer the questions that follow.

Comparison and Contrast in the Real World

Brad Leibov, President, New Chicago Fund, Inc.

Who We Are

Although he entered a community college with little motivation, Brad Leibov was inspired to succeed with the help of a school instructor. Brad earned a bachelor's degree from a four-year university and eventually got his master's degree in urban planning and policy. He now owns his own company that helps to revitalize inner-city commercial areas. The flowing paragraph describes how Brad's company restored a special service area (SSA), a declining community targeted for improvements.

New Chicago Fund, Inc., is an expert at advising and leading organizations through all the steps necessary to establish an SSA with strong local support. Our experience acting as liaison among various neighborhood groups and individuals affected by an SSA helps us plan for and address the concerns of residents and property owners. In 2005, New Chicago Fund assisted the Uptown Community Development Corporation with establishing an SSA in Uptown, Chicago. Uptown's commercial area was estimated to lose approximately $506 million annually in consumer expenditures to neighboring commercial districts and suburban shopping centers. Community leaders recognized that Uptown's sidewalks were uninviting with litter, hazardous with unshoveled snow, and unappealing in the lack of pedestrian-friendly amenities found in neighboring commercial districts. The Uptown SSA programs funded the transformation of the commercial area. The sidewalks are regularly cleaned and are litter-free. People no longer have to walk around uncleared snow mounds and risk slipping on the ice because maintenance programs provide full-service clearing. Additionally, SSA funds provided new pedestrian-friendly amenities such as benches, trash receptacles, flower planters, and street-pole banners. The Uptown area is now poised for commercial success.

Vocabulary development

liaison: someone who acts as a communication link

hazardous: dangerous

amenities: attractive features

receptacles: containers

poised: in this sense, ready; also means natural and balanced, relaxed

1. Double-underline the **topic sentence**.
2. What subjects are being contrasted?

3. What is the purpose of the paragraph?

4. What are the points of contrast?

Student Comparison / Contrast Paragraph

Said Ibrahim

Eyeglasses vs. Laser Surgery: Benefits and Drawbacks

Although both eyeglasses and laser surgery can address vision problems successfully, each approach has particular benefits and drawbacks. Whereas one pair of eyeglasses is reasonably priced in comparison with laser surgery, eyeglass prescriptions often change over time, requiring regular lens replacements. As a result, over the wearer's lifetime, costs of eyeglasses can exceed $15,000. On the positive side, an accurate lens prescription results in clear vision with few or no side effects. Furthermore, glasses of just the right shape or color can be a great fashion accent. In contrast to eyeglasses, laser vision correction often has to be done only once. Consequently, although the costs average $2,500 per eye, the patient can save thousands of dollars over the following years. On the downside, some recipients of laser surgery report difficulties seeing at night, dry eyes, or infections. Fortunately, these problems are fairly rare. The final advantage of laser surgery applies to those who are happy to forgo the fashion benefits of eyeglasses. Most laser-surgery patients no longer have to wear any glasses other than sunglasses until later in life. At that point, they may need reading glasses. All in all, we are fortunate to live in a time when there are many good options for vision correction. Choosing the right one is a matter of carefully weighing the pros and cons of each approach.

1. Double-underline the **topic sentence**.

2. Is the **purpose** of the paragraph to help readers make a decision, to help them understand the subjects better, or both?

3. Underline and number **each point of contrast** in the sample paragraph. Then, give each parallel, or matched, point the same number.

4. Which organization (point by point or whole to whole) does Ibrahim use?

5. Circle the **transitions** in the paragraph.

Vocabulary development

laser: a concentrated beam of light; in this case it is used to reshape part of the eye

reasonably: not excessively

forgo: go without

Professional Comparison/Contrast Essay

Mark Twain

Two Ways of Seeing a River

Born Samuel Langhorne Clemens, Mark Twain (1835–1910) is one of America's most admired writers, praised as much for his storytelling as for his humor and wit. He was also a sharp observer of society and politics, and he was known to criticize racial inequality, political corruption, and other injustices.

Twain, a native of Missouri, discovered his love for writing while working as a typesetter and editorial assistant at a local newspaper. Later, he took a job as a river pilot's apprentice. Among the many books Twain was to publish in the following years were *Tom Sawyer* (1876), *Huckleberry Finn* (1884), and *Life on the Mississippi* (1883), from which the following excerpt was taken.

In this essay, Twain paints a vivid picture of the Mississippi River and describes an upsetting change to this picture that occurred during his time as a pilot's apprentice.

Vocabulary development

mastered: had become skilled in

trifling: small; of little importance

majestic: great; dignified

hue: color; tint

solitary: single

conspicuous: clearly visible

opal: a gemstone that, typically, is made up of many colors

Now when I had mastered the language of this water and had come to 1 know every trifling feature that bordered the great river as familiarly as I knew the letters of the alphabet, I had made a valuable acquisition. But I had lost something, too. I had lost something which could never be restored to me while I lived. All the grace, the beauty, the poetry, had gone out of the majestic river! I still kept in mind a certain wonderful sunset which I witnessed when steamboating was new to me. A broad expanse of the river was turned to blood; in the middle distance the red hue brightened into gold, through which a solitary log came floating, black and conspicuous; in one place a long, slanting mark lay sparkling upon the water; in another the surface was broken by boiling, tumbling rings that were as many-tinted as an opal; where the ruddy flush was faintest was a smooth spot that was covered with graceful circles and radiating lines, ever so delicately traced; the shore on our left was densely wooded, and the somber shadow that fell from this forest was broken in one place by a long, ruffled trail that shone like silver; and high above the forest wall a clean-stemmed dead tree waved a single leafy bough that glowed like a flame in the unobstructed splendor that was flowing from the sun. There were graceful curves, reflected images, woody heights, soft distances, and over the whole scene, far and near, the dissolving lights drifted steadily, enriching it every passing moment with new marvels of coloring.

2   I stood like one bewitched. I drank it in, in a speechless rapture. The world was new to me and I had never seen anything like this at home. But as I have said, a day came when I began to cease from noting the glories and the charms which the moon and the sun and the twilight wrought upon the river's face; another day came when I ceased altogether to note them. Then, if that sunset scene had been repeated, I should have looked upon it without rapture and should have commented upon it inwardly after this fashion: "This sun means that we are going to have wind tomorrow; that floating log means that the river is rising, small thanks to it; that slanting mark on the water refers to a bluff reef which is going to kill somebody's steamboat one of these nights, if it keeps on stretching out like that; those tumbling 'boils' show a dissolving bar and a changing channel there; the lines and circles in the slick water over yonder are a warning that that troublesome place is shoaling up dangerously; that silver streak in the shadow of the forest is the 'break' from a new snag and he has located himself in the very best place he could have found to fish for steamboats; that tall dead tree, with a single living branch, is not going to last long, and then how is a body ever going to get through this blind place at night without the friendly old landmark?"

3   No, the romance and beauty were all gone from the river. All the value any feature of it had for me now was the amount of usefulness it could furnish toward compassing the safe piloting of a steamboat. Since those days, I have pitied doctors from my heart. What does the lovely flush in a beauty's cheek mean to a doctor but a "break" that ripples above some deadly disease? Are not all her visible charms sown thick with what are to him the signs and symbols of hidden decay? Does he ever see her beauty at all, or doesn't he simply view her professionally and comment upon her unwholesome condition all to himself? And doesn't he sometimes wonder whether he has gained most or lost most by learning his trade?

1.   Double-underline the **thesis statement**.

2.   What type of organization does this essay use (point by point or whole to whole)?

3.   Why do you suppose Twain's perceptions of the river changed?

4.   How is the writing in the "before" and "after" sections of the essay similar? How is it different?

Vocabulary development

ruddy: rosy

radiating: extending outward

somber: sad

bough: limb

unobstructed splendor: unblocked (view of) beauty

marvels: wonderful things

bewitched: under a spell; fascinated

rapture: joy; ecstasy

wrought: caused to appear

bluff reef: a type of sandbar that is difficult to see and, therefore, dangerous to boats

yonder: in the distance

shoaling up: becoming shallow

snag: a tree or tree part in the water; it can damage boats

compassing: enabling; providing direction for

break: a wave (in this case)

unwholesome: unhealthy

Write Your Own Comparison and Contrast

Write a comparison/contrast paragraph or essay on one of the following topics or on one of your own choice. For help, refer to the How to Write Comparison and Contrast checklist on page 143.

COLLEGE

- Describe similarities and differences between high school and college, and give examples.

- If you are still deciding on a major area of study, see if you can sit in on a class or two from programs that interest you. Then, compare and contrast the classes. If this process helped you decide on a program, explain the reasons for your choice.

WORK

- Compare a job you liked with one you did not like, and give reasons for your views.

- Have you had experience working for both a bad supervisor and a good one? If so, compare and contrast their behaviors, and explain why you preferred one supervisor to another.

EVERYDAY LIFE

- Compare your life now with the way you would like it to be in five years.

- Participate in a cleanup effort in your community, and then compare and contrast how the area looked before the cleanup with how it looked afterward.

CHECKLIST: HOW TO WRITE COMPARISON AND CONTRAST

STEPS	DETAILS
☐ Narrow and explore your topic. See Chapter 2.	• Make the topic more specific. • Prewrite to get ideas about the narrowed topic.
☐ Write a topic sentence (paragraph) or thesis statement (essay). See Chapter 3.	• State the main point you want to make in your comparison/contrast.
☐ Support your point. See Chapter 3.	• Come up with points of comparison/ contrast and with details about each one.
☐ Write a draft. See Chapter 4.	• Make a plan that sets up a point-by-point or whole-to-whole comparison/contrast. • Include a topic sentence (paragraph) or thesis statement (essay) and all the support points.
☐ Revise your draft. See Chapter 4.	• Make sure it has *all* the Four Basics of Good Comparison and Contrast. • Make sure you include transitions to move readers smoothly from one subject or comparison/contrast point to the next.
☐ Edit your revised draft. See Chapters 14 through 17.	• Correct errors in grammar, spelling, word use, and punctuation.

12

Cause and Effect

Writing That Explains Reasons or Results

Understand What Cause and Effect Are

A **cause** is what made an event happen. An **effect** is what happens as a result of the event.

Four Basics of Good Cause and Effect

1. The main point reflects the writer's purpose: to explain causes, effects, or both.
2. If the purpose is to explain causes, the writing presents real causes.
3. If the purpose is to explain effects, it presents real effects.
4. It gives readers detailed examples or explanations of the causes or effects.

In the following paragraph, the numbers and colors correspond to the Four Basics of Good Cause and Effect.

1 Although the thought of writing may be a source of stress for college students, researchers have recently found that it can also be a potent stress reliever. In the winter of 2008, during a time when many people catch colds or the flu or experience other symptoms of ill health, two psychologists conducted an experiment with college students to find out if writing could have positive effects on their minds and/or their bodies. After gathering a large group of college students, a mix of ages, genders, and backgrounds, the

✓ LearningCurve For extra practice in the skills covered in this chapter, visit: bedfordstmartins.com/rwinteractive.

psychologists explained the task. The students were asked to write for only 2 minutes, on two consecutive days, about their choice of three different kinds of experiences: a traumatic experience, a positive experience, or a neutral experience (something routine that happened). The psychologists did not give more detailed directions about the kinds of experiences, rather just a bad one, a good one, or one neither good nor bad. A month after collecting the students' writing, the psychologists interviewed each of the students and asked them to report any symptoms of ill health, such as colds, flu, headaches, or lack of sleep. **3** What the psychologists found was quite surprising. **4** Those students who had written about emotionally charged topics, either traumatic or positive, all reported that they had been in excellent health, avoiding the various illnesses that had been circulating in the college and the larger community. The students who had chosen to write about routine, day-to-day things that didn't matter to them reported the ill health effects that were typical of the season, such as colds, flu, poor sleep, and coughing. From these findings, the two psychologists reported that writing about things that are important to people actually has a positive effect on their health. Their experiment suggests the value to people of regularly recording their reactions to experiences, in a journal of some sort. If writing can keep you well, it is worth a good try. The mind-body connection continues to be studied because clearly each affects the other.

You use cause and effect in many situations.

COLLEGE   In a nutrition course, you are asked to identify the consequences (effects) of poor nutrition.

WORK   Sales are down in your group, and you have to explain the cause.

EVERYDAY   You explain to your child why a certain behavior is not
LIFE   acceptable by warning him or her about the negative effects of that behavior.

In college, writing assignments might include the words *discuss the causes (or effects) of*, but they might also use phrases such as *explain the results of, discuss the impact of,* and *how did* X *affect* Y? In all these cases, use the strategies discussed in this chapter.

Main Point in Cause and Effect

The **main point** introduces causes, effects, or both. Here is an example of a topic sentence for a paragraph:

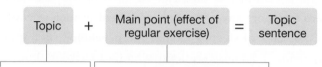

Regular exercise improves cardiovascular health.

Remember that the main point for an essay can be a little broader than one for a paragraph (see pages 148–49).

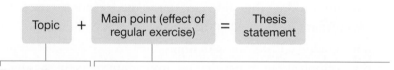

Regular exercise provides more physical and mental benefits than any medication could offer.

Whereas the topic sentence focuses on just one major benefit of regular exercise, the thesis statement considers multiple benefits.

NOTE: When you are writing about causes and effects, make sure that you do not confuse something that happened before an event with a real cause or something that happened after an event with a real effect. For example, if you have pizza on Monday and get the flu on Tuesday, eating the pizza is not the cause of the flu just because it happened before you got the flu, nor is the flu the effect of eating pizza. You just happened to get the flu the next day.

Support in Cause and Effect

The paragraph and essay models on pages 148–49 use the topic sentence (paragraph) and thesis statement (essay) from the Main Point section of this chapter. Both models include the **support** used in all cause-effect writing: statements of cause or effect backed up by detailed explanations or examples. In the essay plan, however, the major support points (statements of cause/effect) are topic sentences for individual paragraphs.

Organization in Cause and Effect

Cause and effect can be organized in a variety of ways, depending on your purpose. (For more on the different orders of organization, see pages 42–43.)

MAIN POINT	PURPOSE	ORGANIZATION
The "Occupy" protests of 2011 brought attention to the economic difficulties faced by low- and middle-income citizens.	to explain the effects of the protests	order of importance, saving the most important effect for last
A desire to remain at a protest site for an extended period led "Occupy" protesters to create miniature towns, with food service, libraries, and more.	to describe the places where protesters camped out	space order
The "Occupy" protests in New York City inspired other protests throughout the country.	to describe the spread of the protest movement over time	time order

NOTE: If you are explaining both causes and effects, you would present the causes first and the effects later.

Use **transitions** to move readers smoothly from one cause to another, or from one effect to another, or from causes to effects. Because cause and effect can use any method of organization depending on your purpose, the following list shows just a few of the transitions you might use.

Common Transitions in Cause and Effect

also	more important/serious cause or effect
as a result	most important/serious cause or effect
because	one cause/effect; another cause or effect
the final cause or effect	a primary cause; a secondary cause
the first, second, third cause or effect	a short-term effect; a long-term effect

PARAGRAPHS VS. ESSAYS IN CAUSE AND EFFECT

For more on the important features of cause and effect, see the Four Basics of Good Cause and Effect on page 144.

Paragraph Form

Topic sentence	Regular exercise improves cardiovascular health.
Support 1 (cause 1 or effect 1)	One benefit of exercise is that it strengthens the heart. Like any other muscle, the heart becomes stronger with use, and is able to pump blood through the body more efficiently. The result can be lower blood pressure, reducing the risk of heart disease.
Support 2 (cause 2 or effect 2)	Another benefit of exercise is that it lessens the toll that excessive weight can take on the heart. In seriously overweight individuals, the strain of carrying extra pounds can cause the heart to enlarge, interfering with its ability to pump blood. By losing weight through exercise and dietary changes, people can reduce the burden on their hearts and also their cardiovascular risk.
Support 3 (cause 3 or effect 3)	The most important cardiovascular benefit of exercise is that it lowers the risk of heart disease. As previously noted, exercise can reduce blood pressure and strain on the heart, both risk factors for heart attack, stroke, and heart failure. In addition, it can lower levels of "bad" cholesterol while raising levels of "good" cholesterol. Controlling bad cholesterol is important because when there is too much of this substance in the blood, it can build up on artery walls, causing reduced blood flow.
Concluding sentence	Regular and vigorous aerobic exercise is the best way to reap these cardiovascular benefits, but even a brisk walk a few times a week is better than no activity at all.

Main Point: Often, narrower for a paragraph than for an essay: While the topic sentence (paragraph) focuses on just one major benefit of exercise, the thesis statement (essay) considers multiple benefits.

Support for the Main Point (Statements of Cause or Effect)

Detailed Explanations or Examples of Cause/Effect Statements: Usually, 1 to 3 sentences per statement for paragraphs and 3 to 8 sentences per statement for essays.

Conclusion

Essay Form

Most people know how hard it is to start and stick with an exercise program. However, there is a good reason to build **[Thesis statement]** amount of physical activity into Regular exercise provides more physical and mental benefits than any medication could offer.

First, exercise helps people achieve and maintain a healthy weight. A nutriti **[Topic sentence 1 (cause 1 or effect 1)]** is not excessive in calories has a grea weight loss than exercise does. How exercise—ideally, interspersed throughout the day—can make an important contribution. For instance, people trying to lose weight might walk to work or to other destinations instead of driving. Or, they might take the stairs to their office instead of the elevator. If the **[Topic sentence 2 (cause 2 or effect 2)]** at the end of the day, so much the b up, all these efforts can make a diff

Second, exercise boosts mood and energy levels. For example, exercise causes the

body to release endorphins, chemicals that give us a sense of well-being, even happiness. Accordingly, exercise can help reduce stress and combat depression. In addition, because exercise can make people look and feel more fit, it can improve their self-esteem. Finally, by improving strength and endurance, **[Topic sentence 3 (cause 3 or effect 3)]** gives individuals more energy to go ab lives.

The most important benefit of exercise is that it can help prevent disease. For example, exercise can improve the body's use of insulin and, as noted earlier, help people maintain a healthy weight. Therefore, it can help prevent or control diabetes. Additionally, exercise can lower the risk of heart attacks, strokes, and heart failure. For instance, exercise strengthens the heart muscle, helping it pump blood more efficiently and reducing high blood pressure, a heart disease risk factor. Also, exercise can

lower levels of "bad" cholesterol while raising levels of "good" cholesterol. Controlling levels of bad cholesterol is important because when there is too much of this substance in the blood, it can build up in the walls of arteries, possibly blocking blood flow. Finally, some research suggests that regular exercise can reduce the risk of certain cancers, including breast, colon, and lung cancer.

[Concluding paragraph] In my own life, exercise has made a huge difference. Before starting a regular exercise program, I was close to needing prescription medications to lower my blood pressure and cholesterol. Thanks to regular physical activity, however, both my blood pressure and cholesterol levels are now in the normal range, and I have never felt better. Every bit of time spent at the gym or exchanging a ride in an elevator for a walk up the stairs has been well worth it.

Read and Analyze Cause and Effect

After you read each of the selections below, answer the questions that follow.

Cause and Effect in the Real World

Mary LaCue Booker, Singer, Actor

School Rules

Mary LaCue Booker studied both nursing and psychology in college before attending the competitive American Academy of Dramatic Arts in Los Angeles. Later, as the chair of the fine arts department in a Georgia middle school, Mary began writing rap songs to help motivate her students. Mary now has three CDs under her stage name La Q, and she has acted in the movie *We Must Go Forward,* about African American history. Mary writes songs, motivational speeches, and screenplays. Below are some lyrics from one of La Q's hit songs.

Now get this, now get this, now get this.
If ya wanna be cool, obey the rules
Cause if ya don't, it's your future you lose.
I'm a school teacher from a rough school.
I see students every day breakin' the rules.
Here comes a new boy with a platinum grill
Makin' trouble, ringin' the fire drill.

There goes anotha' fool wanna run the school,
Breakin' all the damn school rules.
Runnin' in the halls, writin' graffiti on the walls,
Tellin' a lie without blinkin' an eye,
Usin' profanity, pleadin' insanity,
Callin' names, causin' pain,

Joinin' gangs like it's fame,
Dissin' the teacha and each otha.
Regardless of color, they're all sistas and brothas.

Now get this, now get this, now get this, now get this.
Boys and girls are skippin' class,
Cause they late with no hall pass.
They wanna have their say, and that's okay,
But they're outta their minds if they wanna have their way.

Now get this, now get this, now get this.
If ya wanna be free, school's not the place ta be.
But if ya wanna degree, you gotta feel me.
So if you wanna be cool, obey the rules
Cause if ya don't, it's your future you lose.

1.   What is La Q's **purpose**?

2.   What are the **effects** of breaking the rules?

3.   Underline the **causes** that lead to these effects.

4.   With a partner, or as a class, translate this rap into formal English.

Student Cause/Effect Paragraph

Caitlin Prokop

A Difficult Decision with a Positive Outcome

Caitlin Prokop wrote the following essay as she was preparing to begin her studies at Brevard Community College in Florida. Later, she went on to pursue a degree in elementary education at the University of Hawaii. She was inspired to write this essay by her parents. Caitlin understands the balance between inspiration and revision in writing and offers this advice: "Follow what the brain is telling the hand. Let it flow. If you cannot write about the topic that is given, put yourself in someone else's shoes and then write. Let your thoughts flow; then, revise and edit to get the finished copy."

When my mother made the decision to move back to New York, I made the choice to move in with my dad so that I could finish high school. This decision affected me in a positive way because I graduated with my friends, built a better relationship with my father, and had the chance to go to college without leaving home. Graduating with my friends was very important to me because I have known most of them since we were in kindergarten. It was a journey through childhood that we had shared, and I wanted to finish it with them. Accomplishing the goal of graduating from high school with my close friends, those who accompanied me through school, made me a stronger and more confident person. Another good outcome of my difficult decision was the relationship I built with my dad. We never saw eye to eye when I lived with both of my parents. For example, we stopped talking for five months because I always sided against him

TIP For advice on building your vocabulary, visit the Student Site at bedfordstmartins .com/ realwritingbrief.

with my mom. Living together for the past five years has made us closer, and I cherish that closeness we have developed. Every Thursday is our day, a day when we talk to each other about what is going on in our lives, so that we will never again have a distant relationship. A third good outcome of my decision is that I can go to Brevard Community College, which is right down the street. In high school, I had thought that I would want to go away to college, but then I realized that I would miss my home. By staying here, I have the opportunity to attend a wonderful college that is preparing me for transferring to a four-year college and finding a good career. I have done some research and believe I would like to become a police officer, a nurse, or a teacher. Through the school, I can do volunteer work in each of these areas. Right now, I am leaning toward becoming a teacher, based on my volunteer work in a kindergarten class. There, I can explore what grades I want to teach. In every way, I believe that my difficult decision was the right one, giving me many opportunities that I would not have had if I had moved to a new and unfamiliar place.

Vocabulary development

accompany: to be with; to go with

cherish: to value highly

1. Double-underline the **topic sentence**.
2. Does Caitlin write about causes or effects?
3. Circle the **transitions** Caitlin uses to move readers from one point to the next.
4. Does Caitlin's paragraph include the Four Basics of Good Cause and Effect? Why or why not?
5. Have you made a difficult decision that turned out to be a good one? Why and how?

Vocabulary development

epiphany: a sudden understanding or insight

contention: conflict; displeasure

bashful: shy

disdain: contempt; hatred

relatively: in comparison with (in this case) other times

exclusively: only

Professional Cause / Effect Essay

Kristen Ziman

Bad Attitudes and Glowworms

Kristen Ziman is a commander with the Aurora Police Department in Aurora, Illinois, and a columnist for the *Beacon News*. She holds a B.A. in criminal justice management from Aurora University and an M.A. in criminal justice / organizational leadership from Boston University. In addition to writing for the *Beacon News*, Ziman regularly posts to her blog, *Think Different*.

In the following essay, Ziman discusses how keeping a positive attitude helps people maintain control over their lives.

1   In my third-grade classroom there was a poster on the wall that read:

I wish I were a glowworm,

A glowworm's never glum.

'Cuz how can you be grumpy

When the sun shines out your bum!

2   I didn't understand what that poem meant until I was in my twenties, and I had an epiphany about attitude. I was partnered with a veteran officer, and two hours into our eight-hour shift, I began to realize that there was not a single thing he enjoyed about his job or his life. Being assigned to ride with me was also a source of contention for him, and he wasn't bashful about telling me so.

3   I found his disdain for life odd—especially given the fact that it was a beautiful summer day and the few calls we answered were relatively uneventful. As we patrolled the streets, I visualized a dark cloud exclusively over his head in contrast to the sunshine surrounding the rest of us, and I laughed out loud as the glowworm poem popped into my head. It was at that moment that I started to understand the effect our attitude has on our entire existence.

4   Throughout my life, I have been bombarded with lessons about attitude. It's not what happens to us in life, but the way we respond that makes a difference. If you can't change a situation, you must change the way you see the situation. I understand these lessons on an intellectual level, but conceptually, there are times I find it difficult to find the light when darkness seems to be so overwhelming.

5   As I gained more experience as a police officer, I began to understand how the metamorphosis from an optimist to a pessimist occurs. I became distrusting of other human beings, though not without reason. I had been lied to, spit on, and physically attacked while doing my job. I saw the evil human beings did to one another and started to become suspicious of motives all around me. There was a moment when I quietly challenged my decision to make this my career, and I felt my own dark cloud begin to hover.

6   Because I've always been very analytical and self-aware [by my own estimation], I started to pay attention to the negativity of my coworkers, and it suddenly became clear that the miserable ones seemed to feed off each other like vultures. They gravitated towards one another because they validated each other's thoughts and beliefs. They were always victims, and they effortlessly found someone else to blame for all that was wrong. Never did they stop to look in the proverbial mirror and ask themselves if they might be part of the problem.

7   My favorite book is *Man's Search for Meaning* by Viktor Frankl. In his book, Frankl writes about his experiences in the concentration camps of

Vocabulary development

conceptually: in abstract or emotional terms, as opposed to factual terms

overwhelming: bordering on unbearable

metamorphosis: transformation

motives: reasons for people's actions

hover: to float in the air above something

analytical: given to studying things carefully

gravitated towards: were drawn to

validated: confirmed; supported

proverbial: related to a proverb or common saying. ("Look at yourself in the mirror" is a common saying.)

endure: to survive; to make it through a difficult situation

thrive: to be successful

attitudinally: in terms of attitude

self-imposed: put upon oneself

Nazi Germany. He took particular interest in how some of his fellow prisoners seemed to endure and even thrive, while others gave up and laid down to die. From this, he concluded that "everything can be taken from a man but one thing: the last of human freedom is to choose one's attitude in any given set of circumstances—to choose one's own way."

We all struggle in some way with things that are completely out of our control. But the way we gain control over these things—even if only attitudinally—is where our freedom lies. We don't have to experience torture in a concentration camp to apply Frankl's teachings to our own lives. We each have the freedom to make choices that liberate us from our self-imposed prisons. 8

If Frankl's story doesn't motivate you to choose the way you look at things, maybe you need to surround yourselves with more glowworms. 9

1. Double-underline the **thesis statement**.

2. Does this essay present causes, effects, or both? Explain how you came to your conclusion.

3. Does this essay follow the Four Basics of Good Cause and Effect (p. 144)? Why or why not?

Write Your Own Cause and Effect

Write a cause/effect paragraph or essay on one of the following topics or on one of your own choice. For help, refer to the How to Write Cause and Effect checklist on page 155.

COLLEGE

- Write about the causes, effects, or both of not studying for an exam.

- If you have chosen a major or program of study, explain the factors that led to your decision. Or, explain how you think this choice will shape your future.

WORK

- Write about the causes, effects, or both of stress at work.

- Identify a friend or acquaintance who has been successful at work. Write about the factors behind this person's success.

■ Try to fill in this blank: "_____ changed my life." Your response can be an event, an interaction with a particular person, or anything significant to you. It can be something positive or negative. After you fill in the blank, explain how and why this event, interaction, or time had so much significance.

■ Arrange to spend a few hours at a local soup kitchen or food pantry, or on another volunteer opportunity that interests you. (You can search online for volunteer opportunities in your area.) Write about how the experience affected you.

CHECKLIST: HOW TO WRITE CAUSE AND EFFECT

STEPS	DETAILS
☐ **Narrow and explore your topic.** See Chapter 2.	• Make the topic more specific. • Prewrite to get ideas about the narrowed topic.
☐ **Write a topic sentence (paragraph) or thesis statement (essay).** See Chapter 3.	• State your subject and the causes, effects, or both that your paper will explore.
☐ **Support your point.** See Chapter 3.	• Come up with explanations/examples of the causes, effects, or both.
☐ **Write a draft.** See Chapter 4.	• Make a plan that puts the support points in a logical order. • Include a topic sentence (paragraph) or thesis statement (essay) and all the supporting explanations/examples.
☐ **Revise your draft.** See Chapter 4.	• Make sure it has *all* the Four Basics of Good Cause and Effect. • Make sure you include transitions to move readers smoothly from one cause/effect to the next.
☐ **Edit your revised draft.** See Chapters 14 through 17.	• Correct errors in grammar, spelling, word use, and punctuation.

13

Argument

Writing That Persuades

Understand What Argument Is

Argument is writing that takes a position on an issue and gives supporting evidence to persuade someone else to accept, or at least consider, the position. Argument is also used to convince someone to take (or not take) an action.

Four Basics of Good Argument

1 It takes a strong and definite position.

2 It gives good reasons and supporting evidence to defend the position.

3 It considers opposing views.

4 It has enthusiasm and energy from start to finish.

In the following paragraph, the numbers and colors correspond to the Four Basics of Good Argument.

4
Argument is enthusiastic and energetic.

1 Even though I write this blog post on an 88-degree day, I am truly glad that I stopped using my air conditioner, and I urge you to follow my lead. **2** For one thing, going without air conditioning can save a significant amount of money. Last summer, this strategy cut my electricity costs by nearly $2,000, and I am on my way to achieving even higher savings this summer. For another thing, living without air conditioning reduces humans' effect on the environment. Agricultural researcher Stan Cox estimates that air conditioning creates 300 million tons of carbon dioxide (CO_2) emissions each year. This amount, he says, is the equivalent of every U.S. household buying an additional car and driving it 7,000 miles annually. Because CO_2 is one of the greenhouse gases responsible for trapping heat in our atmosphere, reducing CO_2 emissions is essential to curbing climate change. The final reason for going without air conditioning is that it is actually pretty comfortable. The key to staying cool is keeping the blinds down on south-facing windows during the day. It is also a good idea to open windows throughout the home for cross ventilation while turning on ceiling fans to improve air circulation. **3** Although some people argue that using fans is just as bad as switching on the air conditioner, fans use far less electricity. In closing, let me make you a promise: The sooner you give up air conditioning, the sooner you will get comfortable with the change—and the sooner you and the planet will reap the rewards.

Knowing how to make a good argument is one of the most useful skills you can develop.

COLLEGE	You argue for or against makeup exams for students who do not do well the first time.
WORK	You need to leave work an hour early one day a week for twelve weeks to take a course. You persuade your boss to allow you to do so.
EVERYDAY LIFE	You try to negotiate a better price on an item you want to buy.

In college, writing assignments might include questions or statements such as the following: *Do you agree or disagree with* _____? *Defend or refute* _____. *Is* _____ *fair and just?* In all these cases, use the strategies discussed in this chapter.

Main Point in Argument

Your **main point** in argument is the position you take on the issue (or topic) about which you are writing. When you are free to choose an issue, choose something that matters to you. When you are assigned an issue, try to find some part of it that matters to you.

In argument, the topic sentence (in a paragraph) or thesis statement (in an essay) usually includes the issue/topic and your position about it. Here is an example of a topic sentence for a paragraph:

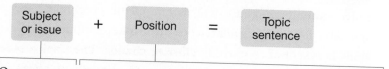

Our company should make regular contributions to local food banks.

Remember that the main point for an essay can be a little broader than one for a paragraph (see pages 160–61).

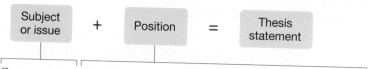

Our company should become more active in supporting charities.

Whereas the topic sentence focuses on just one type of charitable organization, the thesis statement sets up a discussion of different ways to help different charities.

Support in Argument

The paragraph and essay models on pages 160–61 use the topic sentence (paragraph) and thesis statement (essay) from the Main Point section of this chapter. Both models include the **support** used in all argument writing: the **reasons** for the writer's position backed up by **evidence**. In the essay model, however, the major support points (reasons) are topic sentences for individual paragraphs.

TYPES OF EVIDENCE

- **FACTS:** Statements or observations that can be proved. Statistics — real numbers from actual studies — can be persuasive factual evidence.

- **EXAMPLES:** Specific information or experiences that support your position.

- **EXPERT OPINIONS:** The opinions of people considered knowledgeable about your topic because of their educational or work background, their research into the topic, or other qualifications. It is important to choose these sources carefully. For example, an economics professor might be very knowledgeable about the possible benefits and drawbacks of beverage taxes. He or she probably wouldn't be the best source of information on the health effects of soda, however.

- **PREDICTIONS:** Forecasts of the possible outcomes of events or actions. These forecasts are the informed views of experts, not the best guesses of nonexperts.

TESTING EVIDENCE

- Consider your audience's view of the issue. Are audience members likely to agree with you, to be uncommitted, or to be hostile? Then, make sure your evidence would be convincing to a typical member of your audience.

- Reread your evidence from an opponent's perspective, looking for ways to knock it down. Anticipate your opponent's objections, and include evidence to answer them.

- Do not overgeneralize. Statements about what everyone else does or what always happens are easy to disprove. It is better to use facts (including statistics), specific examples, expert opinions, and informed predictions.

- Make sure you have considered every important angle of the issue.

- Reread the evidence to make sure it provides good support for your position. Also, the evidence must be relevant to your argument.

Organization in Argument

Most arguments are organized by **order of importance**, starting with the least important evidence and saving the most convincing reason and evidence for last. (For more on order of importance, see page 43.)

Use **transitions** to move your readers smoothly from one supporting reason to another. Here are some of the transitions you might use in your argument.

Common Transitions in Argument

above all	more important
also	most important
best of all	one fact / another fact
especially	one reason / another reason
for example	one thing / another thing
in addition	remember
in fact	the first (second, third) point
in particular	worst of all
in the first (second, third) place	

PARAGRAPHS VS. ESSAYS IN ARGUMENT

For more on the important features of argument, see the Four Basics of Good Argument on page 156.

Paragraph Form

Main Point: Often, narrower for a paragraph than for an essay: While the topic sentence (paragraph) focuses on just one type of charitable organization, the thesis statement (essay) sets up a discussion of different ways to help different charities.

Support for the Main Point (Reasons for the Writer's Position)

Evidence to Back Up Each Reason: Usually, 1 to 3 sentences per reason for paragraphs and 3 to 8 sentences per reason for essays.

Conclusion

Topic sentence

Support 1 (reason 1)

Support 2 (reason 2)

Support 3 (reason 3)

Concluding sentence

Our company should make regular contributions to local food banks. The first reason for making these contributions is that, as a food wholesaler, we have the resources to do so. Often, we find that we have a surplus of certain items, such as canned goods and pasta, and it would be a waste not to donate this food to organizations that need it so desperately. We could also donate food that is safe to consume but that we cannot sell to stores or institutions. These items include market-testing products from manufacturers and goods with torn labels. Second, these contributions will improve our image among clients. All other things being equal, grocers, schools, hospitals, and other institutions will be more likely to purchase food from a wholesaler that gives something back to the community than one focused on its financial interests alone. The most important reason for making these contributions is to help our company become a better corporate citizen. Especially in challenging economic times, many people see corporations as heartless, and motivated by profits alone. It is important to show not only clients but also the wider community that we are one of the "good guys." That is, we are willing to do what is right, not only within our organization but also in society. Although some question the need for a donation program, arguing that it would take too much time to organize, the good that will come from the program will far exceed the effort devoted to it.

Essay Form

1

At the last executive meeting, we discussed several possible ways to improve our company's marketing and advertising and to increase employee morale. Since attending the meeting, I have become convinc[ed] **[Thesis statement]** effort would help in those areas [.] Our company should become more active in supporting charities.

First, giving time and money to community organizations is a good way to promote our organization. **[Topic sentence 1 (reason 1)]** This approach has wo[rked for] several of our competitors. For exa[mple,] Industries is well known for spon[soring Little] League teams throughout the city. Its name is on the back of each uniform, and banners promoting Lanse's new products appear on the ball fields. Lanse gets free promotion of these efforts through articles in the local papers, and according to one company source quoted in the Hillsburg Gazette, Lanse's good works in the

2

community have boosted its sales by 5 to 10 percent. Another competitor, Great Deals, has employees serve meals at soup kitchens over the holidays and at least once during the spring or summer. It, too, has gotten great publicity from these efforts, including a spot on a [local TV] news show. It is time for our compan[y to start] **[Topic sentence 2 (reason 2)]** reaping these kinds of benefits.

Second, activities like group volunteering will help employees feel more connected to one another and to their community. Kay Rodriguez, a manager at Great Deals and a good friend of mine, organized the company's group volunteering efforts at the soup kitchens, and she cannot say enough good things about the results. Aside from providing meals to the needy, the volunteering has boosted the morale of Great Deals employees because they understand that they are supporting an important cause in their community. Kay has

3

also noticed that as employees work together at the soup kitchens, they form closer bonds. She says, "Some of these people work on different floors and rarely get to see each other during the work week. Or they just do not have time to talk. But while they work together on the volunteering, I see real connections forming." I know that some members of our executive committee might think it would be too time-consuming to organize companywide volunteering efforts. Kay assures me, however, that this is not the case and that the rewards of such efforts far exceed the costs in time.

The most important reason for supporting charities is that it is the right thing to do. **[Topic sentence 3 (reason 3)]** As a successful business that depends [on the] community for a large share of i[ts] employees, I believe we owe that [community] something in return. If our home city does not thrive, how can we? By giving time and money

4

to local organizations, we provide a real service to people, and we present our company as a good and caring neighbor instead of a faceless corporation that could not care less if local citizens went hungry, had trash and graffiti in their parks, or couldn't afford sports teams for their kids. We could make our commu[nity] **[Concluding paragraph]** proud to have us around.

I realize that our main goal is to run a profitable and growing business. I do not believe, however, that this aim must exclude doing good in the community. In fact, I see these two goals moving side-by-side, and hand-in-hand. When companies give back to local citizens, their businesses benefit, the community benefits, and everyone is pleased by the results.

Read and Analyze Argument

After you read each of the selections below, answer the questions that follow.

Argument in the Real World

Diane Melancon, Oncologist

The Importance of Advance Directives

In part because her family never expected her to pursue a career, Diane Melancon took what she describes as a "curvy path" to her medical degree and her current practice in oncology (the treatment of cancer). After high school, she worked her way through a number of educational programs, earning a certificate in medical assistance from Diman Regional Vocational Technical High School, an A.S. in X-ray technology from Northeastern University, a B.A. from Wellesley College, and an M.D. from Dartmouth Medical School. In her medical practice today, she writes patient assessments and treatment plans. In the following piece, she argues for the importance of advance directives, in which patients spell out how they wish their medical treatment to be handled in life-threatening situations.

Consider these difficult situations: (1) A car accident seriously damages a young man's brain, leaving his family to decide whether or not he should be kept on life support. (2) A patient's cancer is not responding well to chemotherapy. She must decide whether to continue with the therapy, despite its physical and emotional strains, or to receive only care that reduces pain and provides comfort. Nothing will make such decisions any easier for these patients or their families. However, people who are able to provide guidance for their treatment in advance of a medical crisis can help ensure that their wishes are followed, even under the most difficult circumstances. Therefore, everyone should seriously consider preparing advance directives for medical care.

One major reason for preparing advance directives is that they make it clear to care providers, family, and other loved ones which medical measures patients do or do not want to be taken during a health crisis. Directives specify these wishes even after patients are no longer able to do so themselves—because, for example, they have lost consciousness. Advance directives include living wills, legal documents that indicate which life-sustaining measures are acceptable to patients and under what circumstances. These measures include the use of breathing aids, such as ventilators, and of feeding aids, such as tube-delivered nutrition. Living wills may also indicate a point at which a patient wishes to receive only comfort care, as opposed to aggressive treatment. Furthermore, living wills may specify whether patients wish to receive cardiopulmonary resuscitation if their heart and breathing stop. Finally, through a legal document known as a medical power of attorney, patients may select another person to make medical decisions on their behalf if they become incapable of doing so themselves. All of these parts of advance directives help reduce the risk that patients' wishes will be overlooked or contradicted during any point of the treatment process.

Another important reason for preparing advanced directives is that they can reduce stress and confusion in the delivery of care. Ideally, patients should complete these directives while they are still relatively healthy in mind and body and capable of giving thoughtful and informed instructions for their own medical care. In contrast, waiting until a health problem is far advanced can increase the difficulty and stress of making medical decisions; at this point, patients and their loved ones may be feeling too overwhelmed to think carefully through the various options. In the worst-case scenario, patients may have moved beyond the ability to contribute to medical decisions at all. In such cases, family members and others close to patients may be forced to make their own judgments about which treatments should or should not be given, possibly resulting in disagreements and confusion. However, when patients have made their preferences clear in advance, care delivery moves more smoothly for them and everyone else.

Some people may believe that advance directives are too depressing to think about or that they are even unnecessary. They may take the attitude "Let's cross that bridge when we come to it." However, as has been noted, by the time the bridge is in sight it might already be too late. Although making advance plans for life-threatening medical situations can be difficult and emotional, avoiding such planning can create more stress for patients and their loved ones. Worse, it may mean that the patients' true wishes are never known or acted upon.

1. Double-underline the **thesis statement**.
2. Circle the **transitions** that introduce the different reasons supporting the argument.
3. Underline the part of the essay that presents an opposing view.
4. Does this essay follow the Four Basics of Good Argument (p. 156)? Why or why not?

The next two student essays argue about the wisdom of using social media, like Facebook and Twitter, as educational aids in college. Read both essays, and answer the questions after the second one.

Vocabulary development

chemotherapy: drug therapy aimed at killing cancer cells

strains: difficulties

sustaining: preserving

ventilators: machines that help with or perform the breathing process

aggressive: powerful

cardiopulmonary resuscitation: a method of restoring someone's heart and lung function in an emergency situation

incapable: unable

contradicted: opposed

scenario: situation

Student Argument Essay 1: "Yes" to Social Media in Education

Jason Yilmaz

A Learning Tool Whose Time Has Come

Efforts to incorporate social media into courses at our college have 1
drawn several complaints. A major objection is that Facebook and Twitter
are distractions that have no place in the classroom. Based on my own experiences, I must completely disagree. Social media, when used intelli-
gently, will get students more involved with their courses and help them be
more successful in college.

In the first place, social media can help students engage deeply with 2
academic subjects. For example, in a sociology class that I took in high
school, the instructor encouraged students to use Twitter in a research assignment. This assignment called for us to record, over one week, the number of times we observed students of different races and ethnic groups
interacting outside of the classroom. Each of us made observations in the
lunch room, in the courtyard where students liked to hang out between
classes, and in other public areas. We tweeted our findings as we did our
research, and in the end, we brought them together to write a group report.
The Twitter exchanges gave each of us new ideas and insights. Also, the
whole process helped us understand what a research team does in the real
world.

In the second place, social media are a good way for students to get 3
help and support outside of class. As a commuter student with a job, it is
hard for me to get to my instructors' office hours, let alone meet with other
students. Therefore, I would value Facebook groups that would let me post
questions about assignments and other homework and get responses from
instructors and other students. Also, I would be able to form online study
groups with classmates.

Finally, social networking can make students feel more confident and 4
connected. In the sociology course where I used Twitter, I found that other
students valued and respected the information that I shared, just as I valued
their contributions. Also, all of us felt like we were "in this together"—an
uncommon experience in most classrooms. I have heard that feeling connected to other students and to the larger college community can make
people less likely to drop out, and I believe it.

New things often scare people, and the use of social media in education 5
is no exception. However, I would hate to see fears about social media get
in the way of efforts to make students more engaged with and successful in
college. We owe it to students to overcome such fears.

Vocabulary development

incorporate: to add; to bring into

objection: an argument against something

distractions: things that draw attention away from something else

engage: to become involved in

Student Argument Essay 2: "No" to Social
Media in Education

Shari Beck

A Classroom Distraction—and Worse

1   Last week, I saw the campus newspaper's story about new efforts to incorporate Twitter, Facebook, and other social media into courses. What did I think about these efforts? To get my answer, I only had to lower the newspaper. Across the table from me was my fourteen-year-old son, whom I'd just told, for the third time, to go upstairs and do his homework. Instead, he was still under the spell of his phone, thumbs flying as he continued to text a friend about who knows what.

2   As you might have guessed already, my answer to my own question is this: Making social media part of a college education is a terrible idea, for a whole lot of reasons.

3   One reason is the distraction factor, illustrated by my phone-addicted son. I am confident that he is not the only person incapable of turning his full attention to any subject when the competition is an incoming or outgoing text message, or anything happening on a computer screen. Supporters of the college's social-media initiative say that students will benefit from discussing course material on Facebook or Twitter. I am concerned, however, that such discussions—when and if they ever take place—would quickly go off-topic, turning into social exchanges. Also, participants' attention could easily wander to other links and news flashes.

4   Another reason I am opposed to social media in education is that students' postings on Facebook or Twitter might compromise their privacy. I am not confident that all teachers will educate students about the importance of limiting the personal information that they make available in public forums. Tech-savvy students probably know how to maximize their privacy settings, but I doubt that all students do.

5   My biggest concern is that students will use social media to cheat. According to proponents of the social-media initiative, one of the biggest educational advantages of Facebook and Twitter is that students can exchange information and form study groups. But it is also possible that they will share answers to homework or test questions or take credit for information posted or tweeted by others. They may not realize that such information theft is plagiarism—something that could cause them to fail a course, or worse. In responding to a 2011 survey by the Pew Research Center, 55 percent of college presidents said that student plagiarism had increased over the previous ten years. Of those who reported this increase, 89 percent said computers and the Internet played "a major role." It would be a shame

Vocabulary
development
spell: a state
of being en-
chanted or
fascinated by
something
initiative: a
program or
process
compromise:
to interfere
with
savvy: knowl-
edgeable or
sophisticated
plagiarism:
using other
people's words
as your own

to make this growing problem even worse through programs like the college's social-media initiative.

From where I sit—once again, across the table from my phone-distracted son—the disadvantages of this initiative far outweigh the benefits. I plan to send an e-mail opposing it to the Student Affairs Office. First, though, I'm taking my son's phone away for the night.

6

1. Double-underline the **thesis statement** in both essays.

2. Underline the **reasons** for the position taken in each essay.

3. Does each essay follow the Four Basics of Good Argument (p. 156)? Give examples to support your answer.

4. Write down at least one additional support point/reason that one of the authors might have included. Then, describe the types of evidence that could be used to back up this support point.

Write Your Own Argument

Write an argument paragraph or essay on one of the following topics or on one of your own choice. For help, refer to the How to Write Argument checklist on page 167.

COLLEGE

- Take a position on a controversial issue on your campus. If you need help coming up with topics, you might consult the campus newspaper.

- Argue for or against the use of standardized tests or placement tests. Make sure to research different positions on the tests to support your argument and address opposing views. One Web site you might consult is standardizedtests.procon.org.

WORK

- Argue for something that you would like to get at work, such as a promotion, a raise, or a flexible schedule. Explain why you deserve what you are asking for, and give specific examples.

- Argue for an improvement in your workplace, such as the addition of a bike rack, new chairs in the break room, or a place to swap books or magazines. Make sure your request is reasonable in cost and will be beneficial to a significant number of employees.

EVERYDAY LIFE

- Take a position on a controversial issue in your community.

- Choose a community organization that you belong to, and write about why it is important. Try to persuade your readers to join.

CHECKLIST: HOW TO WRITE ARGUMENT

STEPS	DETAILS
☐ Narrow and explore your topic. See Chapter 2.	• Make the topic more specific. • Prewrite to get ideas about the narrowed topic.
☐ Write a topic sentence (paragraph) or thesis statement (essay). See Chapter 3.	• State your position on your topic.
☐ Support your point. See Chapter 3.	• Come up with reasons and evidence to back up your position.
☐ Write a draft. See Chapter 4.	• Make a plan that puts the reasons in a logical order. • Include a topic sentence (paragraph) or thesis statement (essay) and all the reasons and supporting evidence.
☐ Revise your draft. See Chapter 4.	• Make sure it has *all* the Four Basics of Good Argument. • Make sure you include transitions to move readers smoothly from one reason to the next.
☐ Edit your revised draft. See Chapters 14 through 17.	• Correct errors in grammar, spelling, word use, and punctuation.

14

Basic Grammar

An Overview

This chapter reviews the basic sentence elements that you will need to understand to find and fix most grammatical errors.

NOTE: In the examples in this chapter, subjects are underlined once, and verbs are underlined twice.

The Parts of Speech

There are seven basic parts of speech:

1. **Noun:** names a person, place, thing, or idea

   Jaime dances.

2. **Pronoun:** replaces a noun in a sentence. *He, she, it, we,* and *they* are pronouns.

   She dances.

3. **Verb:** tells what action the subject does or links a subject to another word that describes it.

   Jaime **dances.**   [The verb *dances* is what the subject, Jaime, does.]

   She **is** a dancer.   [The verb *is* links the subject, Jaime, to a word that describes her, *dancer.*]

✓ **LearningCurve** For extra practice in the skills covered in this chapter, visit: bedfordstmartins.com/rwinteractive.

4. **Adjective:** describes a noun or a pronoun

    Jaime is **thin**.   [The adjective *thin* describes the noun *Jaime*.]

    She is **graceful**.   [The adjective *graceful* describes the pronoun *She*.]

5. **Adverb:** describes an adjective, a verb, or another adverb. Adverbs often end in *-ly*.

    Jaime is **extremely** graceful.   [The adverb *extremely* describes the adjective *graceful*.]

    She practices **often**.   [The adverb *often* describes the verb *practices*.]

    Jaime dances **quite** beautifully.   [The adverb *quite* describes another adverb, *beautifully*.]

6. **Preposition:** connects a noun, pronoun, or verb with information about it. *Across, around, at, in, of, on,* and *out* are prepositions (there are many others).

    Jaime practices **at** the studio.   [The preposition *at* connects the verb *practices* with the noun *studio*.]

7. **Conjunction:** connects words to each other. An easy way to remember the seven common conjunctions is to connect them in your mind to **FANBOYS**: *for, and, nor, but, or, yet, so.*

    The studio is expensive **but** good.

The Basic Sentence

A **sentence** is the basic unit of written communication. A complete sentence in written standard English must have these three elements:

-   A **subject**
-   A **verb**
-   A **complete thought**

Subjects

The **subject** of a sentence is the person, place, or thing, or idea that a sentence is about. The subject of a sentence can be a noun or a pronoun. For a list of common pronouns, see pages 204–205.

To find the subject, ask yourself, **Whom or what is the sentence about?**

> **PERSON AS SUBJECT**   Isaac arrived last night.
>
> [***Whom*** is the sentence about? *Isaac*]

> **THING AS SUBJECT**   The restaurant has closed.
>
> [***What*** is the sentence about? The *restaurant*]

A **compound subject** consists of two or more subjects joined by *and, or,* or *nor.*

> **TWO SUBJECTS**   Kelli and Kate love animals of all kinds.

> **SEVERAL SUBJECTS**   The baby, the cats, and the dog play well together.

The subject of a sentence is *never* in a **prepositional phrase**, a word group that begins with a preposition and ends with a noun or pronoun, called the **object of a preposition**.

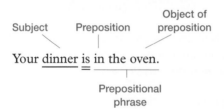

PREPOSITION	OBJECT	PREPOSITIONAL PHRASE
from	the bakery	from the bakery
to	the next corner	to the next corner
under	the table	under the table

Common Prepositions

about	after	among	because of	below
above	against	around	before	beneath
across	along	at	behind	beside

between	in	of	past	until
by	inside	off	since	up
down	into	on	through	upon
during	like	out	to	with
except	near	outside	toward	within
for	next to	over	under	without
from				

See if you can identify the subject of the following sentence.

One of my best friends races cars.

Although you might think that the word *friends* is the subject, it isn't. *One* is the subject. The word *friends* cannot be the subject because it is in the prepositional phrase *of my best friends*. When you are looking for the subject of a sentence, cross out the prepositional phrase.

PREPOSITIONAL PHRASE CROSSED OUT

One ~~of the students~~ won the science prize.

The rules ~~about the dress code~~ are very specific.

TIP For practices on sentence basics, visit *Exercise Central* at bedfordstmartins .com/realwriting.

Verbs

Every sentence has a **main verb**, the word or words that tell what the subject does or that link the subject to another word that describes it. There are three kinds of verbs: action verbs, linking verbs, and helping verbs.

ACTION VERBS

An **action verb** tells what action the subject performs.

To find the main action verb in a sentence, ask yourself: **What action does the subject perform?**

ACTION VERBS   The band played all night.

The alarm rings loudly.

LINKING VERBS

A **linking verb** connects (links) the subject to another word or group of words that describes the subject. Linking verbs show no action. The most common linking verb is *be* (*am, is, are,* and so on). Other linking verbs, such as *seem* and *become*, can usually be replaced by a form of the verb *be*, and the sentence will still make sense.

To find linking verbs, ask yourself: **What word joins the subject and the words that describe the subject?**

LINKING VERBS   The bus is late.

My new shoes look shiny. (My new shoes are shiny.)

The milk tastes sour. (The milk is sour.)

Some words can be used as either action verbs or linking verbs, depending on how the verb is used in a particular sentence.

ACTION VERB   Justine smelled the flowers.

LINKING VERB   The flowers smelled wonderful.

Common Linking Verbs

FORMS OF BE	FORMS OF SEEM AND BECOME	FORMS OF SENSE VERBS
am	seem, seems, seemed	look, looks, looked
are		appear, appears, appeared
is	become, becomes, became	
was		smell, smells, smelled
were		taste, tastes, tasted
		feel, feels, felt

HELPING VERBS

A **helping verb** joins the main verb in a sentence to form the **complete verb** (also known as a verb phrase—the main verb and all of its helping verbs). The helping verb is often a form of the verb *be, have,* or *do.* A sentence may have more than one helping verb along with the main verb.

Helping verb	+	Main verb	=	Complete verb

Sharon <u>was listening</u> to the radio as <u>she</u> <u>was studying</u> for the test.
[The helping verb is *was*; the complete verbs are *was listening* and *was studying.*]

<u>I</u> <u>am saving</u> my money for a car.

<u>Colleen</u> <u>might have borrowed</u> my sweater.

<u>You</u> <u>must pass</u> this course before taking the next one.

<u>You</u> <u>should stop</u> smoking.

Common Helping Verbs

FORMS OF *BE*	FORMS OF *HAVE*	FORMS OF *DO*	OTHER
am	have	do	can
are	has	does	could
been	had	did	may
being			might
is			must
was			should
were			will
			would

Complete Thoughts

A **complete thought** is an idea, expressed in a sentence, that makes sense by itself, without additional words. An incomplete thought leaves readers wondering what's going on.

INCOMPLETE THOUGHT	because my alarm did not go off
COMPLETE THOUGHT	<u>I</u> <u>was</u> late because my alarm did not go off.

INCOMPLETE THOUGHT	the people who won the lottery
COMPLETE THOUGHT	The <u>people</u> who won the lottery <u>were</u> old.

To determine whether a thought is complete, ask yourself: **Do I have to ask a question to understand?**

INCOMPLETE THOUGHT	in my wallet
	[You would have to ask a question to understand, so it is not a complete thought.]
COMPLETE THOUGHT	My <u>ticket</u> <u>is</u> in my wallet.

Six Basic English Sentence Patterns

In English, there are six basic sentence patterns, some of which you have just worked through in this chapter. Although there are other patterns, they build on these six.

1. **Subject-Verb (S-V).** This pattern is the most basic one, as you have already seen.

    S   V
    <u>Babies</u> <u>cry</u>.

2. **Subject-Linking Verb-Noun (S-LV-N)**

    S   LV   N
    <u>They</u> <u>are</u> children.

3. **Subject-Linking Verb-Adjective (S-LV-ADJ)**

    S   LV   ADJ
    <u>Parents</u> <u>are</u> tired.

4. **Subject-Verb-Adverb (S-V-ADV)**

    S   V   ADV
    <u>They</u> <u>sleep</u> poorly.

5. **Subject-Verb-Direct Object (S-V-DO).** A *direct object* directly
   receives the action of the verb.

   > S   V   DO
   >
   > <u>Teachers</u> <u><u>give</u></u> tests.   [The *tests* are given.]

6. **Subject-Verb-Direct Object-Indirect Object.** An *indirect object*
   does not directly receive the action of the verb.

   > S   V   DO   IO
   >
   > <u>Teachers</u> <u><u>give</u></u> tests to students.   [The *tests* are given; the *students* are not.]

   This pattern can also have the indirect object before the direct object.

   > S   V   IO   DO
   >
   > <u>Teachers</u> <u><u>give</u></u> students tests.

15

The Four Most Serious Errors

Fragments, Run-Ons, Subject-Verb Agreement Problems, and Verb-Tense Problems

This chapter of the book focuses first on four grammar errors that people most often notice.

THE FOUR MOST SERIOUS ERRORS

1. Fragments
2. Run-ons and comma splices
3. Problems with subject-verb agreement
4. Problems with verb form and tense

If you can edit your writing to correct these four errors, your grades will improve.

NOTE: In the examples in this chapter, subjects are underlined once, and verbs are underlined twice.

Fragments

A **fragment** is a group of words that is missing one or more parts of a complete sentence: a subject, a verb, or a complete thought.

SENTENCE	I was hungry, so I ate some cold pizza and drank a soda.
FRAGMENT	I was hungry, so I ate some cold pizza. *And drank a soda.*
	[*And drank a soda* contains a verb (*drank*) but no subject.]

LearningCurve For extra practice in the skills covered in this chapter, visit: bedfordstmartins.com/rwinteractive.

176

To find fragments in your own writing, look for the five trouble spots in this chapter. When you find a fragment in your own writing, you can usually correct it in one of two ways.

BASIC WAYS TO CORRECT A FRAGMENT

- Add what is missing (a subject, a verb, or both).
- Attach the fragment to the sentence before or after it.

1. Fragments That Start with Prepositions

Whenever a preposition starts what you think is a sentence, check for a subject, a verb, and a complete thought. If the group of words is missing any of these three elements, it is a fragment. You can correct the fragment by connecting it to the sentence either before or after it.

FINDING AND FIXING FRAGMENTS:
Fragments That Start with a Preposition

Find

I pounded as hard as I could. (Against) the door.

1. **Circle** any preposition that starts a word group.
2. **Ask:** Does the word group have a subject? *No.* A verb? *No.* **Underline** any subject, and **double-underline** any verb.
3. **Ask:** Does the word group express a complete thought? *No.*
4. If the word group is missing a subject or verb or does not express a complete thought, it is a fragment. *This word group is a fragment.*

Fix

I pounded as hard as I could. Against the door.

5. **Correct the fragment** by joining it to the sentence before or after it.

For a lot of common prepositions, see pages 170–71.

2. Fragments That Start with Dependent Words

A **dependent word** (also called a **subordinating conjunction**) is the first word in a dependent clause.

A dependent clause cannot be a sentence because it does not express a complete thought, even though it has a subject and a verb. Whenever a dependent word starts what you think is a sentence, stop to check for a subject, a verb, and a complete thought.

Common Dependent Words

after	if/if only	until
although	now that	what (whatever)
as/as if/as though	once	when (whenever)
as long as/as soon as	since	where (wherever)
because	so that	whether
before	that	which
even if/even though	though	while
how	unless	who/whose

You can correct a fragment by connecting it to the sentence before or after it. If the dependent clause is joined to the sentence after it, put a comma after the dependent clause.

| **FINDING AND FIXING FRAGMENTS:** |
| Fragments That Start with a Dependent Word |

↓

Find

(Because) a job search is important. People should take the time to do it correctly.

1. **Circle** any dependent word that starts either word group.
2. **Ask:** Does the word group beginning with a dependent word have a subject? Yes. A verb? Yes. **Underline** any subject, and **double-underline** any verb.
3. **Ask:** Does this word group express a complete thought? No.
4. If the word group is missing a subject or verb or does not express a complete thought, it is a fragment. *This word group is a fragment.*

↓

Fix

Because a job search is important,/ People should take the time to do it correctly.

5. **Correct the fragment** by joining it to the sentence before or after it. Add a comma if the dependent word group comes first.

3. Fragments That Start with *-ing* Verb Forms

An ***-ing* verb form** (also called a **gerund**) is the form of a verb that ends in *-ing: walking, writing, running.* Sometimes, an *-ing* verb form introduces a fragment. When an *-ing* verb form starts what you think is a sentence, stop and check for a subject, a verb, and a complete thought.

You can correct this type of fragment either by adding whatever sentence elements are missing (usually a subject and a helping verb) or by connecting the fragment to the sentence before or after it. Usually, you will need to put a comma before or after the fragment to join it to the complete sentence.

FINDING AND FIXING FRAGMENTS:
Fragments That Start with *-ing* Verb Forms

Find

I was running as fast as I could. (Hoping) to get there on time.

1. **Circle** any *-ing* verb that starts a word group.
2. **Ask:** Does the word group have a subject? *No.* A verb? *Yes.*
   Underline any subject, and **double-underline** any verb.
3. **Ask:** Does the word group express a complete thought? *No.*
4. If the word group is missing a subject or a verb or does not express a
   complete thought, it is a fragment. *This word group is a fragment.*

Fix

I was running as fast as I could, Hoping to get there on time.

I was hoping
I was running as fast as I could. ~~Hoping~~ to get there on time.

5. **Correct the fragment** by joining it to the sentence before or after it.
   Alternative: Add the missing sentence elements.

---

4. Fragments That Start with *to* and a Verb

If a word group begins with *to* and a verb, it must have another verb; if not,
it is not a complete sentence. When you see a word group that begins with
to and a verb, first check to see if there is another verb. If there is no other
verb, the word group is a fragment.

To correct a fragment that starts with *to* and a verb, join it to the sentence before or after it, or add the missing sentence elements.

> **FINDING AND FIXING FRAGMENTS:**
> Fragments That Start with *to* and a Verb

Find

Cheri got underneath the car. To change the oil.

1. **Circle** any *to*-plus-verb combination that starts a word group.
2. **Ask:** Does the word group have a subject? *No.* A verb? *Yes.*
   Underline any subject, and **double-underline** any verb.
3. **Ask:** Does the word group express a complete thought? *No.*
4. If the word group is missing a subject or a verb or does not express a complete thought, it is a fragment. *This word group is a fragment.*

Fix

                                        t
Cheri got underneath the car. To change the oil.
                              ^

To change the oil,
Cheri got underneath the car. ~~To change the oil.~~
^

                                    She needed to
Cheri got underneath the car. ~~To~~ change the oil.
                              ^

5. **Correct the fragment** by joining it to the sentence before or after it. If you put the *to*-plus-verb word group first, put a comma after it.
   Alternative: Add the missing sentence elements.

5. Fragments That Are Examples or Explanations

When a group of words gives an example or explanation connected to the previous sentence, stop to check it for a subject, a verb, and a complete thought.

The following words may signal a fragment that is an example or explanation.

TIP *Such as* and *like* do not often begin complete sentences.

especially   for example   like   such as

Correct a fragment that starts with an example or explanation by connecting it to the sentence before or after it. Sometimes, you can add whatever sentence elements are missing (a subject, a verb, or both) instead. When you connect the fragment to a sentence, you may need to change some punctuation. For example, fragments that are examples are often set off by a comma.

FINDING AND FIXING FRAGMENTS:
Fragments That Are Examples or Explanations

Find

Freecycle.org recycles usable items. Such as clothing.

1. **Circle** the word group that is an example or explanation.
2. **Ask:** Does the word group have a subject, a verb, and a complete thought? *No.*
3. If the word group is missing a subject or a verb or does not express a complete thought, it is a fragment. *This word group is a fragment.*

Fix

Freecycle.org recycles usable itemssuch as clothing.

You may need to add some words to correct fragments:

I should list some things on freecycle.org. The sweaters I
could keep others warm
never wear.

4. **Correct the fragment** by joining it to the sentence before or after it or by adding the missing sentence elements.

Run-Ons

A **run-on** is two complete sentences (**independent clauses**) joined incorrectly as one sentence. (For help identifying a complete sentence, see Chapter 14.) There are two kinds of run-ons: **fused sentences** and **comma splices**. A **fused sentence** is two complete sentences joined without any punctuation.

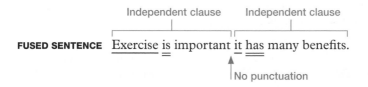

FUSED SENTENCE   Exercise is important it has many benefits.

A **comma splice** is two complete sentences joined by only a comma.

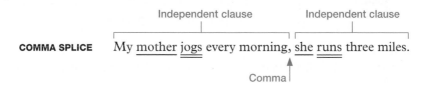

COMMA SPLICE   My mother jogs every morning, she runs three miles.

When you join two sentences, use the proper punctuation.

CORRECTIONS   Exercise is important; it has many benefits.

My mother jogs every morning; she runs three miles.

To find run-ons, focus on each sentence in your writing, one at a time. Once you have found a run-on, there are three ways to correct it.

WAYS TO CORRECT RUN-ONS

1. **Add a period or a semicolon.**

2. **Add a comma and a coordinating conjunction.**

3. **Add a dependent word.**

1. Correct Run-On by Adding a Period or a Semicolon

You can correct run-ons by adding a period to make two separate sentences. After adding the period, capitalize the letter that begins the new sentence. Reread your two sentences to make sure they each contain a subject, a verb, and a complete thought.

RUN-ON **(CORRECTED)**	I interviewed a candidate for a job ̣ S͟he gave me the "dead fish" handshake.

A semicolon (;) can be used instead of a period to join two closely related sentences. Do not capitalize the word that follows a semicolon unless it is the name of a specific person, place, or thing that is usually capitalized—for example, Mary, New York, or the Eiffel Tower.

RUN-ON **(CORRECTED)**	It is important in an interview to hold your head up; it is just as important to sit up straight.

NOTE: The semicolon may be followed by a **conjunctive adverb**—such as *however, indeed, instead, moreover, nevertheless,* and *similarly*—and a comma.

                    Conjunctive
        Semicolon   adverb   Comma
                 \ | /
I stopped by the market; however, it was closed.

FINDING AND FIXING RUN-ONS:
Adding a Period or a Semicolon

↓

Find

Few people know the history of many popular holidays

Valentine's Day is one of these holidays.

1. To see if there are two independent clauses in a sentence, **underline** the subjects, and **double-underline** the verbs.
2. **Ask:** If the sentence has two independent clauses, are they separated by either a period or a semicolon? *No. It is a run-on.*

↓

Fix

Few people know the history of many popular holidays.
Valentine's Day is one of these holidays.
                                                        ^

Few people know the history of many popular holidays;
Valentine's Day is one of these holidays.
                                                        ^

                                                    indeed,
Few people know the history of many popular holidays;
Valentine's Day is one of these holidays.
                                                      ^ ^

3. **Correct** the error by adding a period or a semicolon. The semicolon may
be followed by a conjunctive adverb and a comma.

---

2. Correct Run-On by Adding a Comma and a Coordinating Conjunction

Another way to correct run-ons is to add a comma and a **coordinating
conjunction**: a link that joins independent clauses to form one sentence.
The seven coordinating conjunctions are *and, but, for, nor, or, so, yet.* Some
people remember these words by thinking of **FANBOYS:** *for, and, nor,
but, or, yet, so.*

**RUN-ON
(CORRECTED)**

                                                    , but
Nakeisha was qualified for the job she hurt her
chances by mumbling.   ^

FINDING AND FIXING RUN-ONS:
Using a Comma and / or a Coordinating Conjunction

Find

Foods differ from place to place your favorite treat might

disgust someone from another culture.

1. To see if there are two independent clauses in a sentence, **underline** the
subjects, and **double-underline** the verbs.
2. **Ask:** If the sentence has two independent clauses, are they separated by
either a period or a semicolon? *No. It is a run-on.*

Fix

, and

Foods differ from place to place your favorite treat might disgust

someone from another culture.

3. **Correct** a fused sentence by adding a comma and a coordinating conjunction between the two independent clauses. Correct a comma splice by adding just a coordinating conjunction.

3. Correct Run-On by Adding a Dependent Word

A third way to correct run-ons is to make one of the complete sentences a dependent clause by adding a dependent word (a **subordinating conjunction** or a **relative pronoun**), such as *after, because, before, even though, if, that, though, unless, when, who,* and *which*. (For a more complete list of these words, see the graphic on p. 178.) When the dependent clause is the second clause in a sentence, you usually do not need to put a comma before it unless it is showing contrast.

NOTE: If the dependent clause following the independent clause shows a contrast, a comma is needed.

Many holidays have religious origins, *though some celebrations have moved away from their religious roots.*

DEPENDENT WORDS

after	now that	what(ever)
although	once	when(ever)
as	since	where
because	so that	whether
before	that	which(ever)
even if/though	though	while
how	unless	who
if/if only	until	

RUN-ON
(CORRECTED)   It is important to end an interview on a positive note,/
because
that final impression is what the interviewer will

remember.

You can also put the dependent clause first. When the dependent clause comes first, be sure to put a comma after it.

When the ,
RUN-ON   ~~The~~ interviewer stands the candidate should shake
(CORRECTED)
his or her hand firmly.

FINDING AND FIXING RUN-ONS:
Making a Dependent Clause

Find

Alzheimer's disease is a heartbreaking illness, it causes a steady

decrease in brain capacity.

1. To see if there are two independent clauses in a sentence, **underline** the subjects, and **double-underline** the verbs.
2. **Ask:** If the sentence has two independent clauses, are they separated by a period, a semicolon, or a comma and a coordinating conjunction? *No. It is a run-on.*

Fix

because
Alzheimer's disease is a heartbreaking illness,/it causes a

steady decrease in brain capacity.

3. If one part of the sentence is less important than the other, or if you want to make it so, add a dependent word to the less important part.

NOTE: You can use the word *then* to join two sentences, but if you add it without the correct punctuation or added words, your sentence will be a run-on.

> **COMMA SPLICE**   I picked up my laundry, then I went home.

Correct errors caused by *then* just as you would correct any other run-on.

I picked up my laundry, then I went home.

I picked up my laundry, then I went home.

and
I picked up my laundry, then I went home.

before
I picked up my laundry, then I went home.

Problems with Subject-Verb Agreement

In any sentence, the **subject and the verb must match—or agree**—in number. If the subject is singular (one person, place, or thing), the verb must also be singular. If the subject is plural (more than one), the verb must also be plural.

> **SINGULAR**   The skydiver jumps out of the airplane.
>
> **PLURAL**   The skydivers jump out of the airplane.

Regular Verbs, Present Tense

	SINGULAR		PLURAL
First person	I walk.	} no -s	We walk.
Second person	You walk.		You walk.
Third person	He (she, it) walks.	} all end in -s	They walk.
	Joe walks.		Joe and Alice walk.
	The student walks.		The students walk.

Regular verbs (with forms that follow standard English patterns) have two forms in the present tense: one that ends in -*s* and one that has no ending. The third-person subjects—*he, she, it*—and singular nouns always use the form that ends in -*s*. First-person subjects (*I*), second-person subjects (*you*), and plural subjects use the form with no ending.

To find problems with subject-verb agreement in your own writing, look for five trouble spots that often signal these problems.

1. The Verb Is a Form of *Be, Have,* or *Do*

The verbs *be, have,* and *do* do not follow the rules for forming singular and plural forms; they are **irregular verbs**.

Forms of the Verb *Be*

PRESENT TENSE	SINGULAR	PLURAL
First person	I am	we are
Second person	you are	you are
Third person	she, he, it is	they are
	the student is	the students are

PAST TENSE		
First person	I was	we were
Second person	you were	you were
Third person	she, he, it was	they were
	the student was	the students were

Forms of the Verb *Have,* Present Tense

	SINGULAR	PLURAL
First person	I have	we have
Second person	you have	you have
Third person	she, he, it has	they have
	the student has	the students have

Forms of the Verb *Do*, Present Tense

	SINGULAR	PLURAL
First person	I do	we do
Second person	you do	you do
Third person	she, he, it does	they do
	the student does	the students do

These verbs cause problems for writers who in conversation use the same form in all cases: *He do the cleaning; they do the cleaning.* People also sometimes use the word *be* instead of the correct form of *be: She be on vacation.*

In college and at work, use the correct forms of the verbs *be, have,* and *do* as shown in the charts above.

FINDING AND FIXING PROBLEMS WITH SUBJECT-VERB AGREEMENT:
Making Subjects and Verbs Agree When the Verb Is *Be, Have,* or *Do*

Find

I (am / is / are) a true believer in naps.

1. **Underline** the subject.
2. **Ask:** Is the subject in the first (*I*), second (*you*), or third person (*he*/*she*)? *First person.*
3. **Ask:** Is the subject singular or plural? *Singular.*

Fix

I / is / are) a true believer in naps.

4. **Choose** the verb by matching it to the form of the subject (first person, singular).

2. Words Come between the Subject and the Verb

When the subject and verb are not directly next to each other, it is more difficult to find them to make sure they agree. Most often, either a prepositional phrase or a dependent clause comes between the subject and the verb.

PREPOSITIONAL PHRASE BETWEEN THE SUBJECT AND THE VERB

A **prepositional phrase** starts with a preposition and ends with a noun or pronoun: I took my bag *of books* and threw it *across the room*. (For a list of common prepositions, see pp. 170–71.)

The subject of a sentence is never in a prepositional phrase. When you are looking for the subject of a sentence, you can cross out any prepositional phrases.

**FINDING AND FIXING PROBLEMS
WITH SUBJECT-VERB AGREEMENT:**
Making Subjects and Verbs Agree When They
Are Separated by a Prepositional Phrase

Find

Learners ~~with dyslexia~~ (face / faces) many challenges.

1. **Underline** the subject.
2. **Cross out** any prepositional phrase that follows the subject.
3. **Ask:** Is the subject singular or plural? *Plural.*

Fix

Learners with dyslexia (face)/ faces) many challenges.

4. **Choose** the form of the verb that matches the subject.

DEPENDENT CLAUSE BETWEEN THE SUBJECT AND THE VERB

A **dependent clause** has a subject and a verb, but it does not express a complete thought. When a dependent clause comes between the subject and the verb, it usually starts with the word *who, whose, whom, that,* or *which.*

The subject of a sentence is never in a dependent clause. When you are looking for the subject of a sentence, you can cross out any dependent clauses.

**FINDING AND FIXING PROBLEMS
WITH SUBJECT-VERB AGREEMENT:**
Making Subjects and Verbs Agree When They
Are Separated by a Dependent Clause

Find

The security systems ~~that shopping sites on the Internet provide~~
(is / are) surprisingly effective.

1. **Underline** the subject.
2. **Cross out** any dependent clause that follows the subject. (Look for the words *who, whose, whom, that,* and *which* because they can signal such a clause.)
3. **Ask:** Is the subject singular or plural? *Plural.*

Fix

The security systems that shopping sites on the Internet provide
(is / (are)) surprisingly effective.

4. **Choose** the form of the verb that matches the subject.

---

3. The Sentence Has a Compound Subject

A **compound subject** is two (or more) subjects joined by *and, or,* or *nor.*

And / Or Rule: If two subjects are joined by *and,* use a plural verb. If two subjects are joined by *or* (or *nor*), they are considered separate, and the verb should agree with whatever subject it is closer to.

Plural subject = Plural verb

The teacher *and* her aide grade all the exams.

Subject *or* Singular subject = Singular verb

Either the teacher *or* her aide grades all the exams.

Subject *nor* Plural subject = Plural verb

Neither the teacher *nor* her aides grade all the exams.

**FINDING AND FIXING PROBLEMS
WITH SUBJECT-VERB AGREEMENT:**
Making Subjects and Verbs Agree in a Sentence
with a Compound Subject

Find

Watermelon or cantaloupe (makes / make) a delicious and healthy snack.

1. **Underline** the subjects.
2. **Circle** the word between the subjects.
3. **Ask:** Does that word join the subjects to make them plural or keep them separate? *Keeps them separate.*
4. **Ask:** Is the subject that is closer to the verb singular or plural? *Singular.*

Fix

Watermelon or cantaloupe (makes / make) a delicious and healthy snack.

5. **Choose** the verb form that agrees with the subject that is closer to the verb.

4. The Subject Is an Indefinite Pronoun

An **indefinite pronoun** replaces a general person, place, or thing or a general group of people, places, or things. Indefinite pronouns are often singular, although there are some exceptions, as shown in the chart on the next page.

Remember that the verb of a sentence must agree with the subject of the sentence, and the subject of a sentence is *never in a prepositional phrase or dependent clause.*

Indefinite Pronouns

ALWAYS SINGULAR (USE THE *IS* FORM OF *BE*)		
anybody	everyone	nothing
anyone	everything	one (of)
anything	much	somebody
each (of)	neither (of)	someone
either (of)	nobody	something
everybody	no one	

ALWAYS PLURAL (USE THE *ARE* FORM OF *BE*)	
both	many
few	several

MAY BE SINGULAR OR PLURAL (USE THE *IS* OR *ARE* FORM OF *BE*)		
all	most	some
any	none	

FINDING AND FIXING PROBLEMS WITH SUBJECT-VERB AGREEMENT:
Making Subjects and Verbs Agree When the Subject Is an Indefinite Pronoun

Find

One ~~of my best friends~~ (lives / live) in California.

1. **Underline** the subject.
2. **Cross out** any prepositional phrase or dependent clause that follows the subject.
3. **Ask:** Is the subject singular or plural? *Singular.*

Fix

One of my best friends (lives / live) in California.

4. **Choose** the verb form that agrees with the subject.

5. The Verb Comes before the Subject

In most sentences, the subject comes before the verb. Two kinds of sentences often reverse the usual subject-verb order: questions and sentences that begin with *here* or *there*. To find the subject and verb in these types of sentences, you can turn them around.

Are you excited? / You are excited.

There are four keys on the table. / Four keys are on the table.

**FINDING AND FIXING PROBLEMS
WITH SUBJECT-VERB AGREEMENT:**
Making Subjects and Verbs Agree When
the Verb Comes before the Subject

Find

What classes (is / are) the professor teaching?

There (is / are) two good classes in the music department.

1. If the sentence is a question, **turn the question into a statement**: *The professor (is/are) teaching the classes.*
2. If the sentence begins with *here* or *there,* **turn it around**: *Two good classes (is/are) in the music department.*
3. **Identify** the subject in each of the two new sentences. *It is "professor" in the first sentence and "classes" in the second.*
4. **Ask:** Is the subject singular or plural? *"Professor" is singular; "classes" is plural.*

Fix

What classes (is)/ are) the professor teaching?

There (is /(are) two good classes in the music department.

5. **Choose** the form of the verb in each sentence that matches the subject.

Problems with Verb Tense

Verb tense tells *when* an action happened: in the past, in the present, or in the future. Verbs change their form or use the helping verbs *have, be,* or *will* to indicate different tenses.

PRESENT TENSE	Rick hikes every weekend.
PAST TENSE	He hiked 10 miles last weekend.
FUTURE TENSE	He will hike again on Saturday.

LANGUAGE NOTE: Remember to include needed endings on present-tense and past-tense verbs, even if they are not noticed in speech.

PRESENT TENSE	Nate listens to his new iPod wherever he goes.
PAST TENSE	Nate listened to his iPod while he walked the dog.

Regular Verbs

Most verbs in English are **regular verbs** that follow standard rules about what endings to use to express time.

PRESENT-TENSE ENDINGS: -*S* AND NO ENDING

The **present tense** is used for actions that are happening at the same time that they are being written about (the present) and for things that happen all the time. Present-tense, regular verbs either end in -*s* or have no ending added. Use the -*s* ending when the subject is *he, she, it,* or the name of one person or thing. Use no ending for all other subjects.

Regular Verbs in the Present Tense

	SINGULAR	PLURAL
First person	I jump.	We jump.
Second person	You jump.	You jump.
Third person	She (he, it) jumps.	They jump.
	The child jumps.	The children jump.

REGULAR PAST-TENSE ENDING: *-ED* OR *-D*

The **past tense** is used for actions that have already happened. A *-d* or an *-ed* ending is needed on all regular verbs in the past tense.

	PRESENT TENSE		PAST TENSE	
First person	I live.	I walk.	I lived.	I walked.
Second person	You live.	You walk.	You lived.	You walked.
Third person	He lives.	He walks.	He lived.	He walked.

The past-tense form of regular verbs can also serve as the past participle and be paired with a helping verb such as *have* or *do*. (To learn about when past participles are used, see pp. 201–02.)

PAST TENSE	PAST PARTICIPLE
My kids watched cartoons.	They have watched cartoons before.
George visited his cousins.	He has visited them every year.

Irregular Verbs

Irregular verbs do not follow the simple rules of regular verbs. They show past tense with a change in spelling, or by not changing their spelling. The most common irregular verbs are *be* and *have* (see p. 189). As you write and edit, use the following chart to make sure you use the correct form of irregular verbs.

NOTE: What is called "Present Tense" in the chart below is sometimes called the "base form of the verb."

Irregular Verbs

PRESENT TENSE (BASE FORM OF VERB)	PAST TENSE	PAST PARTICIPLE (USED WITH HELPING VERB)
be (am/are/is)	was/were	been
become	became	become
begin	began	begun
bite	bit	bitten
blow	blew	blown
break	broke	broken
bring	brought	brought
build	built	built
buy	bought	bought
catch	caught	caught
choose	chose	chosen
come	came	come
cost	cost	cost
dive	dived, dove	dived
do	did	done
draw	drew	drawn
drink	drank	drunk
drive	drove	driven
eat	ate	eaten
fall	fell	fallen
feed	fed	fed
feel	felt	felt
fight	fought	fought
find	found	found
fly	flew	flown
forget	forgot	forgotten

PRESENT TENSE (BASE FORM OF VERB)	PAST TENSE	PAST PARTICIPLE (USED WITH HELPING VERB)
get	got	gotten
give	gave	given
go	went	gone
grow	grew	grown
have/has	had	had
hear	heard	heard
hide	hid	hidden
hit	hit	hit
hold	held	held
hurt	hurt	hurt
keep	kept	kept
know	knew	known
lay	laid	laid
lead	led	led
leave	left	left
let	let	let
lie	lay	lain
light	lit	lit
lose	lost	lost
make	made	made
mean	meant	meant
meet	met	met
pay	paid	paid
put	put	put
quit	quit	quit

PRESENT TENSE (BASE FORM OF VERB)	PAST TENSE	PAST PARTICIPLE (USED WITH HELPING VERB)
read	read	read
ride	rode	ridden
ring	rang	rung
rise	rose	risen
run	ran	run
say	said	said
see	saw	seen
seek	sought	sought
sell	sold	sold
send	sent	sent
shake	shook	shaken
show	showed	shown
shrink	shrank	shrunk
shut	shut	shut
sing	sang	sung
sink	sank	sunk
sit	sat	sat
sleep	slept	slept
speak	spoke	spoken
spend	spent	spent
stand	stood	stood
steal	stole	stolen

PRESENT TENSE (BASE FORM OF VERB)	PAST TENSE	PAST PARTICIPLE (USED WITH HELPING VERB)
stick	stuck	stuck
sting	stung	stung
strike	struck	struck, stricken
swim	swam	swum
take	took	taken
teach	taught	taught
tear	tore	torn
tell	told	told
think	thought	thought
throw	threw	thrown
understand	understood	understood
wake	woke	woken
wear	wore	worn
win	won	won
write	wrote	written

Past Participles

A **past participle**, by itself, cannot be the main verb of a sentence. When a past participle is combined with another verb, called a **helping verb**, however, it can be used to make the present perfect tense and the past perfect tense.

Have/Has	+	Past participle	=	Present perfect tense

The **present perfect** tense is used for an action that began in the past and either continues into the present or was completed at some unknown time in the past.

My <u>car</u> <u><u>has stalled</u></u> several times recently.

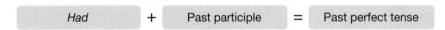

Use *had* plus the past participle to make the **past perfect tense**. The past perfect tense is used for an action that began in the past and ended before some other past action.

My <u>car</u> <u><u>had stalled</u></u> several times before I called the mechanic.

A sentence that is written in the **passive voice** has a subject that does not perform an action. Instead, the subject is acted upon. To create the passive voice, combine a form of the verb *be* with a past participle.

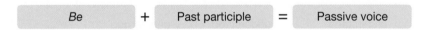

Most sentences should be written in the **active voice**, which means that the subject performs the action.

FINDING AND FIXING VERB-TENSE ERRORS:
Changing from Passive to Active Voice

Find

The game <u>was turned</u> around by (Jo Cortez's touchdown pass).

1. **Underline** the subject, and **double-underline** the verb (in this case, a form of *be* with a past participle).
2. **Circle** any word or words that describe who or what performed the action in the sentence.

Fix

Jo Cortez's touchdown pass
    The game was turned around. ~~by Jo Cortez's touchdown pass.~~
    ^   ^

3. Make the circled words the subject of the sentence, and delete the word *by*.

Jo Cortez's touchdown pass
    The game ~~was~~ turned around. ~~by Jo Cortez's touchdown pass.~~
    ^   ^

4. Change the verb from a past-participle form, using the correct tense.

Jo Cortez's touchdown pass turned the game
    ~~The game was turned~~ around. ~~by Jo Cortez's touchdown pass.~~
    ^   ^

5. Move the former subject so that it receives the action.

NOTE: If you do not have specific information on who or what performed the action, you might use a general word like *someone* or *people*.

Someone left flowers
    ~~Flowers were left~~ on my desk.
    ^

16

Other Grammar and Style Concerns

In addition to checking your writing for the four most serious errors covered in Chapter 15, you will want to be aware of common trouble spots in other areas of grammar and style: pronouns, adjectives and adverbs, modifiers, coordination and subordination, parallelism, sentence variety, and word choice. Matters of punctuation and capitalization are covered in Chapter 17.

Pronouns

A **pronoun** is used in place of a noun or other pronoun mentioned earlier. In most cases, a pronoun refers to a specific noun or pronoun mentioned nearby.

Noun

I picked up my new glasses. They are cool.

Pronoun replacing noun

Common Pronouns			
PERSONAL PRONOUNS	**POSSESSIVE PRONOUNS**	**INDEFINITE PRONOUNS**	
I	my	all	much
me	mine	any	neither (of)

✓ **LearningCurve** For extra practice in the skills covered in this chapter, visit: bedfordstmartins.com/rwinteractive.

PERSONAL PRONOUNS	POSSESSIVE PRONOUNS	INDEFINITE PRONOUNS	
you	your/yours	anybody	nobody
she/he	hers/his	anyone	none (of)
her/him	hers/his	anything	no one
it	its	both	nothing
we	our/ours	each (of)	one (of)
us	our/ours	either (of)	some
they	their/theirs	everybody	somebody
them	their/theirs	everyone	someone
		everything	something
		few (of)	

Check for Pronoun Agreement

A pronoun must agree with (match) the noun or pronoun it refers to in number. It must be either singular (one) or plural (more than one).

If a pronoun is singular, it must also match the noun or pronoun it refers to in gender (*he, she,* or *it*).

> **CONSISTENT**   Magda sold *her* old television set.
>
> [*Her* agrees with *Magda* because both are singular and feminine.]

Watch out for singular, general nouns. If a noun is singular, the pronoun that refers to it must be singular as well.

> *his or her*
> **INCONSISTENT**   Any student can tell you what ~~their~~ least favorite
> course is.
>
> [*Student* is singular, so the plural pronoun *their* must be replaced with the singular pronouns *his* and *her*.]

To avoid using the awkward phrase *his or her*, make the subject plural when you can.

> **CONSISTENT**   Most students can tell you what *their* least favorite
> course is.

Two types of words often cause errors in pronoun agreement: indefinite pronouns and collective nouns.

INDEFINITE PRONOUNS

An **indefinite pronoun** does not refer to a specific person, place, or thing: It is general. Indefinite pronouns often take singular verbs. Whenever a pronoun refers to an indefinite pronoun, check for agreement.

> *his*
> The monks got up at dawn. Everybody had ~~their~~ chores for the day.

Indefinite Pronouns

ALWAYS SINGULAR (USE THE *IS* FORM OF *BE*)		
anybody	everyone	nothing
anyone	everything	one (of)
anything	much	somebody
each (of)	neither (of)	someone
either (of)	nobody	something
everybody	no one	

ALWAYS PLURAL (USE THE *ARE* FORM OF *BE*)		
both	many	
few	several	

MAY BE SINGULAR OR PLURAL (USE THE *IS* OR *ARE* FORM OF *BE*)		
all	most	some
any	none	

NOTE: Although grammatically correct, using the pronoun *he* to refer to an indefinite pronoun such as *everyone* is considered sexist. Here are two ways to avoid this problem:

1. Use *his or her.*

Someone posted *his or her* e-mail address to the Web site.

2. Change the sentence so that the pronoun refers to a plural noun or pronoun.

    Some students posted *their* e-mail addresses to the Web site.

COLLECTIVE NOUNS

A **collective noun** names a group that acts as a single unit. Some common collective nouns are *class*, *committee*, *company*, *family*, *government*, *group*, and *society*.

Collective nouns are usually singular, so when you use a pronoun to refer to a collective noun, it is also usually singular.

                              its
The team had ~~their~~ sixth consecutive win of the season.

If the people in a group are acting as individuals, however, the noun is plural and should be used with a plural pronoun.

                              their
The class brought ~~its~~ papers to read.

Make Pronoun Reference Clear

In an **ambiguous pronoun reference**, the pronoun could refer to more than one noun.

AMBIGUOUS	dirty I put the glass on the shelf, ~~even though it was dirty.~~ [Was the glass dirty? Or was the shelf dirty? The revision makes it clear.]

In a **vague pronoun reference**, the pronoun does not refer clearly to any particular person, place, or thing. To correct a vague pronoun reference, use a more specific noun instead of the pronoun.

VAGUE	the nurse When Tom got to the clinic, ~~they~~ told him it was closed. [Who told Tom the clinic was closed? The revision makes it clear.]

REPETITIOUS PRONOUN REFERENCE

In a **repetitious pronoun reference**, the pronoun repeats a reference to a noun rather than replacing the noun.

The nurse at the clinic ~~he~~ told Tom that it was closed.

The newspaper, ~~it~~ says that the new diet therapy is promising.

Use the Right Type of Pronoun

Three important types of pronouns are **subject pronouns**, **object pronouns**, and **possessive pronouns**. Notice their uses in the following sentences.

Object   Subject
pronoun pronoun

The dog barked at *him,* and *he* laughed.

Possessive
pronoun

As Josh walked out, *his* phone started ringing.

TIP Never put an apostrophe in a possessive pronoun.

Pronoun Types

	SUBJECT	OBJECT	POSSESSIVE
First-person singular/plural	I/we	me/us	my, mine/ our, ours
Second-person singular/plural	you/you	you/you	your, yours/ your, yours
Third-person singular	he, she, it	him, her, it	his, her, hers, its
	who	whom	whose
Third-person plural	they	them	their, theirs
	who	whom	whose

SUBJECT PRONOUNS

Subject pronouns serve as the subject of a verb.

> *You* live next door to a coffee shop.

> *I* opened the door too quickly.

OBJECT PRONOUNS

Object pronouns either receive the action of a verb or are part of a prepositional phrase. (For a list of common prepositions, see pp. 170–71.)

OBJECT OF THE VERB	Jay gave *me* his watch.
OBJECT OF THE PREPOSITION	Jay gave his watch to *me*.

POSSESSIVE PRONOUNS

Possessive pronouns show ownership.

> Dave is *my* uncle.

Three trouble spots make it difficult to know what type of pronoun to use; compound subjects and objects; comparisons; and sentences that need *who* or *whom*.

PRONOUNS USED WITH COMPOUND SUBJECTS AND OBJECTS

A **compound subject** has more than one subject joined by *and* or *or*. A **compound object** has more than one object joined by *and* or *or*.

COMPOUND SUBJECT	Chandler and *I* worked on the project.
COMPOUND OBJECT	My boss gave the assignment to Chandler and *me*.

To decide what type of pronoun to use in a compound construction, try leaving out the other part of the compound and the *and* or *or*. Then, say the sentence aloud to yourself.

Compound subject

~~Joan and~~ (me / (I)) went to the movies last night.

[Think: *I* went to the movies last night.]

Compound object

I will keep that information just between you and (I / (me)).

[*Between you and me* is a prepositional phrase, so an object pronoun, *me*, is required.]

PRONOUNS USED IN COMPARISONS

Using the right type of pronoun in comparisons is particularly important because using the wrong type changes the meaning of the sentence. Editing comparisons can be tricky because they often imply (suggest the presence of) words that are not actually included in the sentence.

Bob trusts Donna more than *I*.

[This sentence means that Bob trusts Donna more than I trust her. The implied words are *trust her*.]

Bob trusts Donna more than *me*.

[This sentence means that Bob trusts Donna more than he trusts me. The implied words are *he trusts*.]

To decide whether to use a subject or object pronoun in a comparison, try adding the implied words and saying the sentence aloud.

The registrar is much more efficient than (us / (we)).

[Think: The registrar is much more efficient than *we are*.]

Susan rides her bicycle more than ((he)/ him).

[Think: Susan rides her bicycle more than *he does*.]

CHOOSING BETWEEN *WHO* AND *WHOM*

Who is always a subject; *whom* is always an object. If a pronoun performs an action, use the subject form *who*. If a pronoun does not perform an action, use the object form *whom*.

> **WHO = SUBJECT**   I would like to know *who* delivered this package.
>
> **WHOM = OBJECT**   He told me to *whom* I should report.

In sentences other than questions, when the pronoun (*who* or *whom*) is followed by a verb, use *who*. When the pronoun (*who* or *whom*) is followed by a noun or pronoun, use *whom*.

> The pianist (who / whom) played was excellent.
> [The pronoun is followed by the verb *played*. Use *who*.]
>
> The pianist (who / whom) I saw was excellent.
> [The pronoun is followed by another pronoun: *I*. Use *whom*.]

Make Pronouns Consistent in Person

Person is the point of view a writer uses — the perspective from which he or she writes. Pronouns may be in first person (*I* or *we*), second person (*you*), or third person (*he, she,* or *it*). (See the chart on p. 208.)

> **INCONSISTENT**   As soon as *a shopper* walks into the store, *you* can tell it is a weird place.
>
> [The sentence starts with the third person (*a shopper*) but shifts to the second person (*you*).]
>
> **CONSISTENT, SINGULAR**   As soon as *a shopper* walks into the store, *he* or *she* can tell it is a weird place.
>
> **CONSISTENT, PLURAL**   As soon as *shoppers* walk into the store, *they* can tell it is a weird place.

Adjectives and Adverbs

Adjectives describe or modify nouns (words that name people, places, things, or ideas) and pronouns (words that replace nouns). They add information about *what kind, which one,* or *how many.*

The *final* exam was today.

It was *long* and *difficult.*

The *three shiny new* coins were on the dresser.

Adverbs describe or modify verbs (words that tell what happens in a sentence), adjectives, or other adverbs. They add information about *how, how much, when, where, why,* or *to what extent.*

MODIFYING VERB	Sharon *enthusiastically* accepted the job.
MODIFYING ADJECTIVE	The *very* young lawyer handled the case.
MODIFYING ANOTHER ADVERB	The team played *surprisingly* well.

Adjectives usually come before the words they modify; adverbs come before or after. You can use more than one adjective or adverb to modify a word.

Choosing between Adjectives and Adverbs

Many adverbs are formed by adding *-ly* to the end of an adjective.

ADJECTIVE	She received a *quick* answer.
ADVERB	Her sister answered *quickly.*

To decide whether to use an adjective or an adverb, find the word being described. If that word is a noun or pronoun, use an adjective. If it is a verb, adjective, or another adverb, use an adverb.

Adjectives and Adverbs in Comparisons

To compare two people, places, or things, use the **comparative** form of adjectives or adverbs. Comparisons often use the word *than.*

Carol ran *faster* than I did.

Johan is *more intelligent* than his sister.

To compare three or more people, places, or things, use the **superlative** form of adjectives or adverbs.

Carol ran the *fastest* of all the women runners.

Johan is the *most intelligent* of the five children.

If an adjective or adverb is short (one syllable), add the endings *-er* to form the comparative and *-est* to form the superlative. Also use this pattern for adjectives that end in *-y* (but change the *-y* to *-i* before adding *-er* or *-est*).

For all other adjectives and adverbs, add the word *more* to make the comparative and the word *most* to make the superlative.

Forming Comparatives and Superlatives

ADJECTIVE OR ADVERB	COMPARATIVE	SUPERLATIVE
ADJECTIVES AND ADVERBS OF ONE SYLLABLE		
tall	taller	tallest
fast	faster	fastest
ADJECTIVES ENDING IN -Y		
happy	happier	happiest
silly	sillier	silliest
OTHER ADJECTIVES AND ADVERBS		
graceful	more graceful	most graceful
gracefully	more gracefully	most gracefully
intelligent	more intelligent	most intelligent
intelligently	more intelligently	most intelligently

Use either an ending (*-er* or *-est*) or an extra word (*more* or *most*) to form a comparative or superlative — not both at once.

J. K. Rowling is the ~~most~~ richest author in the world.

Good, Well, Bad, and Badly

Four common adjectives and adverbs have irregular forms: *good, well, bad,* and *badly.*

Forming Irregular Comparatives and Superlatives

	COMPARATIVE	SUPERLATIVE
ADJECTIVE		
good	better	best
bad	worse	worst
ADVERB		
well	better	best
badly	worse	worst

People often get confused about whether to use *good* or *well. Good* is an adjective, so use it to describe a noun or pronoun. *Well* is an adverb, so use it to describe a verb or an adjective.

ADJECTIVE   She has a *good* job.

ADVERB   He works *well* with his colleagues.

Well can also be an adjective to describe someone's health: I am not *well* today.

Misplaced and Dangling Modifiers

Modifiers are words or word groups that describe other words in a sentence. Modifiers should be near the words they modify; otherwise, the sentence can be confusing or unintentionally funny.

Misplaced Modifiers

A **misplaced modifier**, because it is in the wrong place, describes the wrong word or words.

MISPLACED   Linda saw the White House *flying over Washington, D.C.*

[Was the White House flying over Washington?]

To correct a misplaced modifier, place the modifier as close as possible to the word or words it modifies, often directly before it.

CLEAR   *Flying over Washington, D.C.,* Linda saw the White House.

Four constructions often lead to misplaced modifiers.

1. **Modifiers such as *only, almost, hardly, nearly,* and *just.*** These words need to be immediately before—not just close to—the words or phrases they modify.

    Joanne ~~almost~~ ate _{almost} the whole cake.

    [Joanne actually ate; she did not "almost" eat.]

2. **Modifiers that are prepositional phrases.**

    Jen served punch *in plastic cups* to the seniors. ~~in plastic cups.~~

3. **Modifiers that start with *-ing* verbs.**

    Wearing flip-flops, Javier climbed the mountain. ~~wearing flip-flops.~~

    [The mountain was not wearing flip-flops; Javier was.]

4. **Modifier clauses that start with *who, whose, that,* or *which.***

    The baby *who was crying* on the bus ~~who was crying~~ had curly hair.

    [The bus was not crying; the baby was.]

Dangling Modifiers

A **dangling modifier** "dangles" because the word or word group it modifies is not in the sentence. Dangling modifiers usually appear at the beginning of a sentence and seem to modify the noun or pronoun that immediately follows them, but they are really modifying another word or group of words.

DANGLING   *Rushing to class,* the books fell out of my bag.

                [The books were not rushing to class.]

CLEAR   *Rushing to class,* I dropped my books.

There are two basic ways to correct dangling modifiers. Use the one that makes more sense. One way is to add the word being modified immediately after the opening modifier so that the connection between the two is clear.

Trying to eat a hot dog, *I* ~~my bike~~ swerved *on my bike*.

Another way is to add the word being modified in the opening modifier itself.

    While I was trying
    ~~Trying~~ to eat a hot dog, my bike swerved.

Coordination and Subordination

Joining two sentences with related ideas can make your writing less choppy.

Coordination

In **coordination,** two sentences can be joined with a comma and a coordinating conjunction, a semicolon alone, or a semicolon and a conjunctive adverb.

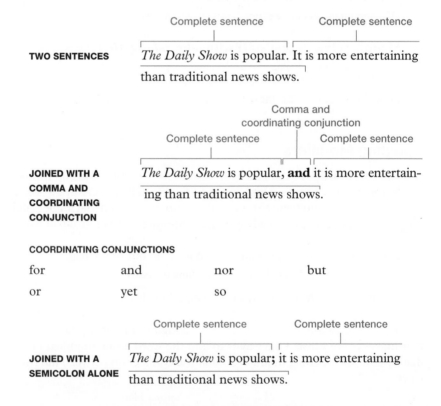

TWO SENTENCES — Complete sentence | Complete sentence

The Daily Show is popular. It is more entertaining than traditional news shows.

JOINED WITH A COMMA AND COORDINATING CONJUNCTION — Comma and coordinating conjunction / Complete sentence | Complete sentence

The Daily Show is popular, **and** it is more entertaining than traditional news shows.

COORDINATING CONJUNCTIONS

for	and	nor	but
or	yet	so	

JOINED WITH A SEMICOLON ALONE — Complete sentence | Complete sentence

The Daily Show is popular; it is more entertaining than traditional news shows.

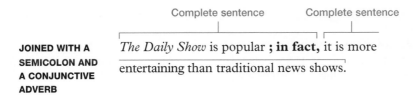

JOINED WITH A SEMICOLON AND A CONJUNCTIVE ADVERB	*The Daily Show* is popular **; in fact,** it is more entertaining than traditional news shows.

CONJUNCTIVE ADVERBS

also	however	moreover
as a result	in addition	still
besides	in fact	then
furthermore	instead	therefore

Subordination

With **subordination,** you put a dependent word (such as *after, although, because,* or *when*) in front of one of the sentences, which then becomes a dependent clause and is no longer a complete sentence.

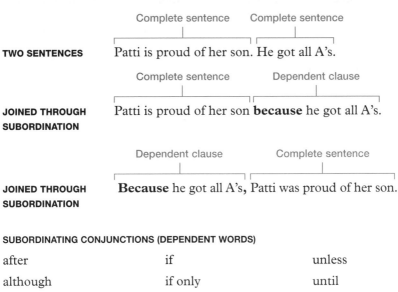

TWO SENTENCES	Patti is proud of her son. He got all A's.
JOINED THROUGH SUBORDINATION	Patti is proud of her son **because** he got all A's.
JOINED THROUGH SUBORDINATION	**Because** he got all A's, Patti was proud of her son.

SUBORDINATING CONJUNCTIONS (DEPENDENT WORDS)

after	if	unless
although	if only	until
as	now that	when
as if	once	whenever
because	since	where
before	so that	while
even if/though		

Parallelism

Parallelism in writing means that similar parts in a sentence have the same structure: Their parts are balanced. When comparing things or listing items in a series, use nouns with nouns, verbs with verbs, and phrases with phrases.

NOT PARALLEL	I enjoy <u>basketball</u> more than <u>playing video games</u>.
	[*Basketball* is a noun, but *playing video games* is a phrase.]
PARALLEL	I enjoy <u>basketball</u> more than <u>video games</u>.
PARALLEL	I enjoy <u>playing basketball</u> more than <u>playing video games</u>.
NOT PARALLEL	Last night, I <u>worked</u>, <u>studied</u>, and <u>was watching</u> television.
	[Verbs must be in the same tense to be parallel. *Was watching* has a different structure from *worked* and *studied*.]
PARALLEL	Last night, I <u>worked</u>, <u>studied</u>, and <u>watched</u> television.
PARALLEL	Last night, I was <u>working</u>, <u>studying</u>, and <u>watching</u> television.
NOT PARALLEL	This weekend, we can go <u>to the beach</u> or <u>walking in the mountains</u>.
	[*To the beach* should be paired with another prepositional phrase: *to the mountains*.]
PARALLEL	This weekend, we can go <u>to the beach</u> or <u>to the mountains</u>.

Certain paired words, called **correlative conjunctions**, link two equal elements and show the relationship between them. Here are the paired words:

both . . . and	neither . . . nor	rather . . . than
either . . . or	not only . . . but also	

Make sure the items joined by these paired words are parallel.

NOT PARALLEL	Bruce wants *both* <u>freedom</u> *and* <u>to be wealthy</u>.
	[*Both* is used with *and*, but the items joined by them are not parallel.]
PARALLEL	Bruce wants *both* <u>freedom</u> *and* <u>wealth</u>.

NOT PARALLEL	He can *neither* <u>fail the course</u> and <u>quitting his job</u> is also impossible.
PARALLEL	He can *neither* <u>fail the course</u> *nor* <u>quit his job</u>.

Sentence Variety

Sentence variety means using different sentence patterns and lengths to give your writing good rhythm and flow. Here are some strategies for achieving more sentence variety in your writing.

Start Some Sentences with Adverbs

Adverbs are words that describe verbs, adjectives, or other adverbs; they often end with -*ly*. As long as the meaning is clear, adverbs can be placed at the beginning of a sentence instead of in the middle. Adverbs at the beginning of a sentence are usually followed by a comma.

ADVERB IN MIDDLE	Stories about haunted houses *frequently* surface at Halloween.
ADVERB AT BEGINNING	*Frequently*, stories about haunted houses surface at Halloween.

Join Ideas Using an *-ing* Verb

One way to combine sentences is to add -*ing* to the verb in the less important of the two sentences and to delete the subject, creating a phrase.

TWO SENTENCES	A pecan roll from our bakery is not a health food. It contains 800 calories.
JOINED WITH -*ING* VERB FORM	*Containing* 800 calories, a pecan roll from our bakery is not a health food.

Join Ideas Using a Past Participle

Another way to combine sentences is to use a past participle (often, a verb ending in -*ed*) to turn the less important of the two sentences into a phrase.

TWO SENTENCES	Henry VIII was a powerful English king. He is *remembered* for his many wives.
JOINED WITH A PAST PARTICIPLE	*Remembered* for his many wives, Henry VIII was a powerful English king.

Join Ideas Using an Appositive

An **appositive** is a noun or noun phrase that renames a noun or pronoun. Appositives can be used to combine two sentences into one.

TWO SENTENCES	Brussels sprouts can be roasted for a delicious flavor. They are a commonly disliked food.
JOINED WITH AN APPOSITIVE	Brussels sprouts, a commonly disliked food, can be roasted for a delicious flavor.

[The phrase *a commonly disliked food* renames the noun *brussels sprouts.*]

Join Ideas Using an Adjective Clause

An **adjective clause** is a group of words with a subject and a verb that describes a noun. An adjective clause often begins with the word *who, which,* or *that,* and it can be used to combine two sentences into one.

TWO SENTENCES	Lauren has won many basketball awards. She is captain of her college team.
JOINED WITH AN ADJECTIVE CLAUSE	Lauren, *who is captain of her college team,* has won many basketball awards.

NOTE: If an adjective clause is an essential part of a sentence, do not put commas around it.

Lauren is an award-winning basketball player who overcame childhood cancer.

[*Who overcame childhood cancer* is an essential part of this sentence.]

Word-Choice Problems

Five common problems with word choice may make it hard for readers to understand your point.

Vague and Abstract Words

Vague and abstract words are too general. They do not give your readers a clear idea of what you mean. Here are some common vague and abstract words.

Vague and Abstract Words

a lot	cute	nice	stuff
amazing	dumb	OK (okay)	terrible
awesome	good	old	thing
bad	great	pretty	very
beautiful	happy	sad	whatever
big	huge	small	young

When you see one of these words or another general word in your writing, replace it with a concrete or more specific word or description. A **concrete** word names something that can be seen, heard, felt, tasted, or smelled. A **specific** word names a particular person or quality. Compare these two sentences:

VAGUE AND ABSTRACT   An old man crossed the street.

CONCRETE AND SPECIFIC   An eighty-seven-year-old priest stumbled along Main Street.

The first version is too general to be interesting. The second version creates a clear, strong image. Some words are so vague that it is best to avoid them altogether.

VAGUE AND ABSTRACT   It is awesome.

[This sentence is neither concrete nor specific.]

Slang

Slang, informal and casual language, should be used only in informal situations. Avoid it when you write, especially for college classes or at work. Use language that is appropriate for your audience and purpose.

SLANG	EDITED
S'all good.	Everything is going well.
Dawg, I don't deserve this grade.	Professor, I don't deserve this grade.

Wordy Language

Too many words can weaken a writer's point.

WORDY	I am not interested *at this point in time.*
EDITED	I am not interested now.
	[The phrase *at this point in time* uses five words to express what could be said in one word: *now.*]

Common Wordy Expressions

WORDY	EDITED
As a result of	Because
Due to the fact that	Because
In spite of the fact that	Although
It is my opinion that	I think (*or just make the point*)
In the event that	If
The fact of the matter is that	(*Just state the point.*)
A great number of	Many
At that time	Then
In this day and age	Now
At this point in time	Now
In this paper I will show that . . .	(*Just make the point; do not announce it.*)
Utilize	Use

Clichés

Clichés are phrases used so often that people no longer pay attention to them. To get your point across and to get your readers' attention, replace clichés with fresh and specific language.

CLICHÉS	EDITED
I cannot *make ends meet.*	I do not have enough money to live on.
My uncle *worked his way up the corporate ladder.*	My uncle started as a shipping clerk but ended up as a regional vice president.
This roll is *as hard as a rock.*	This roll is so hard I could bounce it.

Common Clichés

as big as a house	few and far between	spoiled brat
as light as a feather	hell on earth	starting from scratch
better late than never	last but not least	sweating blood/bullets
break the ice	no way on earth	too little, too late
crystal clear	110 percent	24/7
a drop in the bucket	playing with fire	work like a dog
easier said than done		

Sexist Language

Language that favors one gender over another or that assumes that only one gender performs a certain role is called *sexist.* Such language should be avoided.

SEXIST
: A doctor should politely answer *his* patients' questions.

[Not all doctors are male, as suggested by the pronoun *his.*]

REVISED
: A doctor should politely answer *his or her* patients' questions.
Doctors should politely answer *their* patients' questions.

[The first revision changes *his* to *his or her* to avoid sexism. The second revision changes the subject to a plural noun (*Doctors*) so that a genderless pronoun (*their*) can be used. Usually, it is preferable to avoid *his or her.*]

Punctuation and Capitalization

Commas

To get your intended meaning across to your readers, it is important that you use commas correctly, especially in the following situations.

COMMAS BETWEEN ITEMS IN A SERIES

Use commas to separate the items in a series (three or more items), including the last item in the series, which usually has *and* or *or* before it.

We can *sleep in the car, stay in a motel,* or *camp outside.*

COMMAS BETWEEN COORDINATE ADJECTIVES

Coordinate adjectives are two or more adjectives that independently modify the same noun and are separated by commas.

Conor ordered a *big, fat, greasy* burger.

Note that a comma is not used between the final adjective and the noun it describes.

Conor ordered a *big, fat, greasy,* burger.

Cumulative adjectives describe the same noun but are not separated by commas because they form a unit that describes the noun. You can

---

✓ LearningCurve For extra practice in the skills covered in this chapter, visit: bedfordstmartins.com/rwinteractive.

identify cumulative adjectives because separating them by *and* does not make any sense.

The store is having its *last storewide clearance* sale.

[Putting *and* between *last* and *storewide* and between *storewide* and *clearance* would make an odd sentence: The store is having its *last* and *storewide* and *clearance* sale. The adjectives in the sentence are cumulative adjectives and should not be separated by commas.]

COMMAS IN COMPOUND SENTENCES

A **compound sentence** contains two complete sentences joined by a coordinating conjunction: *and, but, for, nor, or, so, yet.* Use a comma before the joining word to separate the two complete sentences.

I called my best friend, and she agreed to drive me to work.

I asked my best friend to drive me to work, but she was busy.

I can take the bus to work, or I can call another friend.

NOTE: A comma alone cannot separate two sentences. Doing so creates a run-on (see pages 183–88).

COMMAS AFTER INTRODUCTORY WORDS

Use a comma after an introductory word, phrase, or clause. The comma lets your readers know when the main part of the sentence is starting.

INTRODUCTORY WORD: *Yesterday,* I went to the game.

INTRODUCTORY PHRASE: *By the way,* I do not have a babysitter for tomorrow.

INTRODUCTORY CLAUSE: *While I waited outside,* Susan went backstage.

COMMAS AROUND APPOSITIVES AND INTERRUPTERS

An **appositive** comes directly before or after a noun or pronoun and renames it.

Lily, *a senior,* will take her nursing exam this summer.

The prices are outrageous at Beans, *the local coffee shop.*

An **interrupter** is an aside or transition that interrupts the flow of a sentence and does not affect its meaning.

My sister, *incidentally*, has good reasons for being late.

Her child had a fever, *for example*.

COMMAS AROUND ADJECTIVE CLAUSES

An **adjective clause** is a group of words that begins with *who, which*, or *that*; has a subject and a verb; and describes a noun right before it in a sentence.

If an adjective clause can be taken out of a sentence without completely changing the meaning of the sentence, put commas around the clause.

Beans, *which is the local coffee shop*, charges outrageous prices.

I complained to Mr. Kranz, *who is the shop's manager*.

If an adjective clause is essential to the meaning of a sentence, do not put commas around it. You can tell whether a clause is essential by taking it out and seeing if the meaning of the sentence changes significantly, as it would if you took the clauses out of the following examples.

The only grocery store *that sold good bread* went out of business.

Students *who do internships* often improve their hiring potential.

COMMAS WITH QUOTATION MARKS

Quotation marks are used to show that you are repeating exactly what someone said. Use commas to set off the words inside quotation marks from the rest of the sentence.

"Let me see your license," demanded the police officer.

"Did you realize," she asked, "that you were going 80 miles per hour?"

I exclaimed, "No!"

Notice that a comma never comes directly after a quotation mark.

COMMAS IN ADDRESSES

Use commas to separate the elements of an address included in a sentence. However, do not use a comma before a zip code.

My address is 2512 Windermere Street, Jackson, Mississippi 40720.

If a sentence continues after a city-state combination or after a street address, put a comma after the state or the address.

> I moved here from Detroit, Michigan, when I was eighteen.

> I've lived at 24 Heener Street, Madison, since 1989.

COMMAS IN DATES

Separate the day from the year with a comma. If you give just the month and year, do not separate them with a comma.

> My daughter was born on November 8, 2004.

> The next conference is in August 2014.

If a sentence continues after the date, put a comma after the date.

> On April 21, 2013, the contract will expire.

COMMAS WITH NAMES

Put a comma after (and sometimes before) the name of someone being addressed directly.

> Don, I want you to come look at this.

> Unfortunately, Marie, you need to finish the report by next week.

COMMAS WITH *YES* OR *NO*

Put a comma after the word *yes* or *no* in response to a question.

> Yes, I believe that you are right.

Apostrophes

An **apostrophe** (') is a punctuation mark that either shows ownership (*Susan's*) or indicates that a letter has been intentionally left out to form a contraction (*I'm, that's, they're*).

APOSTROPHES TO SHOW OWNERSHIP

Add -'s to a singular noun to show ownership even if the noun already ends in -s.

> *Karen's* apartment is on the South Side.

If a noun is plural and ends in *-s*, just add an apostrophe. If it is plural but does not end in *-s*, add *-'s*.

The *twins'* father was building them a playhouse.
[more than one twin]

The *children's* toys were broken.

The placement of an apostrophe makes a difference in meaning.

My *sister's* six children are at my house for the weekend.
[one sister who has six children]

My *sisters'* six children are at my house for the weekend.
[two or more sisters who together have six children]

Do not use an apostrophe to form the plural of a noun.

Gina went camping with her *sisters* and their children.

All the *highways* to the airport are under construction.

Do not use an apostrophe with a possessive pronoun. These pronouns already show ownership (possession).

Is that bag *yours*?   No, it is *ours*.

Possessive Pronouns

my	his	its	their
mine	her	our	theirs
your	hers	ours	whose
yours			

The single most common error with apostrophes and pronouns is confusing *its* (a possessive pronoun) with *it's* (a contraction meaning "it is").

Whenever you write *it's*, test correctness by replacing it with *it is* and reading the sentence aloud to hear if it makes sense.

APOSTROPHES IN CONTRACTIONS

A **contraction** is formed by joining two words and leaving out one or more of the letters. When writing a contraction, put an apostrophe where the letter or letters have been left out.

She's on her way. = *She is* on her way.

I'll see you there. = *I will* see you there.

Be sure to put the apostrophe in the correct place.

It *doesn't* really matter.

Common Contractions

aren't = are not	I'd = I would, I had
can't = cannot	I'll = I will
couldn't = could not	I'm = I am
didn't = did not	I've = I have
don't = do not	isn't = is not
he'd = he would, he had	it's = it is, it has
he'll = he will	let's = let us
he's = he is, he has	she'd = she would, she had
she'll = she will	won't = will not
she's = she is, she has	wouldn't = would not
there's = there is	you'll = you will
they're = they are	you're = you are
who's = who is, who has	you've = you have

Apostrophes with Letters, Numbers, and Time

Use -'s to make letters and numbers plural. The apostrophe prevents confusion or misreading.

> In Scrabble games, there are more *e*'s than any other letter.
>
> In women's shoes, size *8*'s are more common than size *10*'s.

Use an apostrophe or -'s in certain expressions in which time nouns are treated as if they possess something.

> She took four *weeks*' maternity leave after the baby was born.
>
> This *year*'s graduating class is huge.

Quotation Marks

Quotation marks (" ") always appear in pairs. Quotation marks are used with direct quotations and to set off titles.

Quotation Marks for Direct Quotations

When you write a direct quotation, use quotation marks around the quoted words. Quotation marks tell readers that the words used are exactly what was said or written.

1. "I do not know what she means," I said to my friend Lina.
2. Lina asked, "Do you think we should ask a question?"
3. "Excuse me, Professor Soames," I called out, "but could you explain that again?"
4. "Yes," said Professor Soames. "Let me make sure you all understand."

When you are writing a paper that uses outside sources, use quotation marks to indicate where you quote the exact words of a source.

> We all need to become more conscientious recyclers. A recent editorial in the *Bolton Common* reported, "When recycling volunteers spot-checked bags that were supposed to contain only newspaper,

they found a collection of nonrecyclable items such as plastic candy wrappers, aluminum foil, and birthday cards."

When quoting, writers usually use words that identify who is speaking, such as *I said to my friend Lina* in the first example on the previous page. The identifying words can come after the quoted words (example 1), before them (example 2), or in the middle of them (example 3). Here are some guidelines for capitalization and punctuation.

GUIDELINES FOR CAPITALIZATION AND PUNCTUATION

- Capitalize the first letter in a complete sentence that is being quoted, even if it comes after some identifying words (example 2 on the previous page).

- Do not capitalize the first letter in a quotation if it is not the first word in a complete sentence (*but* in example 3).

- If it is a complete sentence and it is clear who the speaker is, a quotation can stand on its own (second sentence in example 4).

- Identifying words must be attached to a quotation; they cannot be a sentence on their own.

- Use commas to separate any identifying words from quoted words in the same sentence.

- Always put quotation marks after commas and periods. Put quotation marks after question marks and exclamation points if they are part of the quoted sentence.

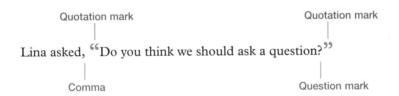

- If a question mark or exclamation point is part of your own sentence, put it after the quotation mark.

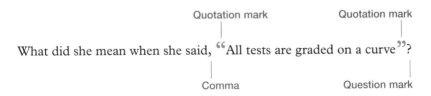

SETTING OFF A QUOTATION WITHIN ANOTHER QUOTATION

Sometimes, when you quote someone directly, part of what that person said quotes words that someone else said or wrote. Put single quotation marks (' ') around the quotation within a quotation so that readers understand who said what.

> Terry told his instructor, "I am sorry I missed the exam, but that is not a reason to fail me for the term. Our student handbook says, 'Students must be given the opportunity to make up work missed for legitimate reasons,' and I have a good reason."

NO QUOTATION MARKS FOR INDIRECT QUOTATIONS

When you report what someone said or wrote but do not use the person's exact words, you are writing an **indirect quotation**. Do not use quotation marks for indirect quotations. Indirect quotations often begin with the word *that*.

> **INDIRECT QUOTATION:** The police told us to move along.
>
> **DIRECT QUOTATION:** "Move along," directed the police.

QUOTATION MARKS FOR CERTAIN TITLES

When you refer to a short work such as a magazine or newspaper article, a chapter in a book, a short story, an essay, a song, or a poem, put quotation marks around the title of the work.

> **NEWSPAPER ARTICLE** "Volunteers Honored for Service"
>
> **SHORT STORY** "The Awakening"
>
> **ESSAY** "Why Are We So Angry?"

Usually, titles of longer works, such as novels, books, magazines, newspapers, movies, television programs, and CDs, are italicized. The titles of sacred books such as the Bible or the Qu'ran are neither underlined nor surrounded by quotation marks.

> **BOOK** *The Good Earth*
>
> **NEWSPAPER** *Washington Post*
>
> [Do not italicize or capitalize the word *the* before the name of a newspaper or magazine, even if it is part of the title: I saw that article in the *New York Times*. But do capitalize *The* when it is the first word in titles of books, movies, and other sources.]

If you are writing a paper with many outside sources, your instructor will probably refer you to a particular system of citing sources. Follow that system's guidelines when you use titles in your paper.

NOTE: Do not enclose the title of a paragraph or an essay that you have written in quotation marks when it appears at the beginning of your paper. Do not italicize it either.

Semicolon ;

SEMICOLONS TO JOIN CLOSELY RELATED SENTENCES

Use a semicolon to join two closely related sentences into one sentence.

> In an interview, hold your head up and do not slouch; it is important to look alert.

> Make good eye contact; looking down is not appropriate in an interview.

SEMICOLONS WHEN ITEMS IN A LIST CONTAIN COMMAS

Use semicolons to separate items in a list that itself contains commas. Otherwise, it is difficult for readers to tell where one item ends and another begins.

> For dinner, Bob ate an order of onion rings; a 16-ounce steak; a baked potato with sour cream, bacon bits, and cheese; a green salad; and a huge bowl of ice cream with fudge sauce.

Because one item, *a baked potato with sour cream, bacon bits, and cheese,* contains its own commas, all items need to be separated by semicolons.

Colon :

COLONS BEFORE LISTS

Use a colon after an independent clause to introduce a list. An independent clause contains a subject, a verb, and a complete thought. It can stand on its own as a sentence.

> The software conference fair featured a vast array of products: financial-management applications, games, educational CDs, college-application programs, and so on.

COLONS BEFORE EXPLANATIONS OR EXAMPLES

Use a colon after an independent clause to let readers know that you are about to provide an explanation or example of what you just wrote.

> The conference was overwhelming: too much hype about too many things.

One of the most common misuses of colons is to use them after a phrase instead of an independent clause. Watch out especially for colons following the phrases *such as* and *for example*.

INCORRECT	Tonya enjoys sports that are sometimes dangerous. For example: white-water rafting, wilderness skiing, rock climbing, and motorcycle racing.
CORRECT	Tonya enjoys sports that are sometimes dangerous: white-water rafting, wilderness skiing, rock climbing, and motorcycle racing.

COLONS IN BUSINESS CORRESPONDENCE AND BEFORE SUBTITLES

Use a colon after a greeting (called a *salutation*) in a business letter and after the standard heading lines at the beginning of a memorandum.

> Dear Mr. Hernandez:
>
> To: Pat Toney
> From: Susan Anker

Colons should also be used before subtitles—for example, "Running a Marathon: The Five Most Important Tips."

Parentheses ( )

Use parentheses to set off information that is not essential to the meaning of a sentence. Parentheses are always used in pairs and should be used sparingly.

> My grandfather's most successful invention (and also his first) was the electric blanket.
>
> When he died (at the age of ninety-six), he had more than 150 patents registered.

Dash --

Dashes can be used like parentheses to set off additional information, particularly information that you want to emphasize. Make a dash by writing or typing two hyphens together. Do not put extra spaces around a dash.

> The final exam--worth 25 percent of your total grade--will be next Thursday.

A dash can also indicate a pause, much like a comma does.

> My uncle went on long fishing trips--without my aunt and cousins.

Hyphen -

HYPHENS TO JOIN WORDS THAT FORM A SINGLE DESCRIPTION

Writers often join two or more words that together form a single description of a person, place, or thing. To join the words, use a hyphen.

> Being a stockbroker is a high-risk career.

> Jill is a lovely three-year-old girl.

When writing out two-word numbers from twenty-one to ninety-nine, put a hyphen between the two words.

> Seventy-five people participated in the demonstration.

HYPHENS TO DIVIDE A WORD AT THE END OF A LINE

Use a hyphen to divide a word when part of the word must continue on the next line.

> Critics accused the tobacco industry of increasing the amounts of nico-tine in cigarettes to encourage addiction and boost sales.

If you are not sure where to break a word, look it up in a dictionary. The word's main entry will show you where you can break the word: *dic • tion • ar • y*. If you still are not confident that you are putting the hyphen in the correct place, do not break the word; write it all on the next line.

Capitalization

If you can remember the following rules, you will avoid the most common errors of capitalization. Capitalize the first letter

- Of every new sentence.
- In names of specific people, places, dates, and things.
- Of important words in titles.

CAPITALIZATION OF SENTENCES

Capitalize the first letter of each new sentence, including the first word of a direct quotation.

> The superintendent was surprised.
>
> He asked, "What is going on here?"

CAPITALIZATION OF NAMES OF SPECIFIC PEOPLE, PLACES, DATES, AND THINGS

The general rule is to capitalize the first letter in names of specific people, places, dates, and things. Do not capitalize a generic (common) name such as *college* as opposed to the specific name: *Carroll State College*. Look at the examples for each group.

People

Capitalize the first letter in names of specific people and in titles used with names of specific people.

SPECIFIC	NOT SPECIFIC
Jean Heaton	my neighbor
Professor Fitzgerald	your math professor
Dr. Cornog	the doctor
Aunt Pat, Mother	my aunt, your mother

The name of a family member is capitalized when the family member is being addressed directly: Happy Birthday, *Mother*. In other instances, do not capitalize: It is my *mother's* birthday.

The word *president* is not capitalized unless it comes directly before a name as part of that person's title: *President* Barack Obama.

Places

Capitalize the first letter in names of specific buildings, streets, cities, states, regions, and countries.

SPECIFIC	NOT SPECIFIC
Bolton Town Hall	the town hall
Arlington Street	our street
Dearborn Heights	my hometown
Arizona	this state
the South	the southern region
Spain	that country

Do not capitalize directions in a sentence.

Drive *south* for five blocks.

Dates

Capitalize the first letter in the names of days, months, and holidays. Do not capitalize the names of the seasons (winter, spring, summer, fall).

SPECIFIC	NOT SPECIFIC
Wednesday	tomorrow
June 25	summer
Thanksgiving	my birthday

Organizations, Companies, and Groups

SPECIFIC	NOT SPECIFIC
Taft Community College	my college
Microsoft	that software company
Alcoholics Anonymous	the self-help group

Languages, Nationalities, and Religions

SPECIFIC	NOT SPECIFIC
English, Greek, Spanish	my first language
Christianity, Buddhism	your religion

The names of languages should be capitalized even if you aren't referring to a specific course.

I am taking psychology and *Spanish*.

Courses

SPECIFIC	NOT SPECIFIC
Composition 101	a writing course
Introduction to Psychology	my psychology course

Commercial Products

SPECIFIC	NOT SPECIFIC
Diet Pepsi	a diet cola
Skippy peanut butter	peanut butter

CAPITALIZATION OF TITLES

When you write the title of a book, movie, television program, magazine, newspaper, article, story, song, paper, poem, and so on, capitalize the first word and all important words. The only words that do not need to be capitalized (unless they are the first word) are *the, a, an,* coordinating conjunctions (*and, but, for, nor, or, so, yet*), and prepositions.

Acknowledgments

Susan Adams. "The Weirdest Job Interview Questions and How to Handle Them." From Forbes.com, June 16, 2011. Reprinted by permission of Forbes Media, LLC. Copyright © 2011.

Janice Castro with Dan Cook and Cristina Garcia. "Spanglish Spoken Here." From *Time*, July 11, 1988. Copyright Time Inc. Reprinted by permission. TIME is a registered trademark of Time Inc. All rights reserved.

Ian Frazier. "How to Operate the Shower Curtain." From *The New Yorker*, January 8, 2007. Reprinted by permission of the author.

Oscar Hijuelos. "Memories of New York City Snow." From *Metropolis Found: New York is Book Country 25th Anniversary Collection* (New York: New York is Book Country, 2003). Copyright © 2003 by Oscar Hijuelos. Reprinted with the permission of The Jennifer Lyons Literary Agency, LLC for the author.

Amanda Jacobowitz. "A Ban on Water Bottles: A Way to Bolster the University's Image." From Student Life. Posted by Amanda Jacobowitz on April 28, 2010. Forum Staff Columnists. Reprinted by permission of the author.

Frances Cole Jones. "Don't Work in a Goat's Stomach." From *The Wow Factor: The 33 Things You Must (And Must Not) Do To Guarantee You Edge In Today's Business World* by Frances Cole Jones. Copyright © 2009, 2010 by Frances Cole Jones. Used by permission of Ballantine Books, a division of Random House, Inc. Any third party use of this material, outside of this publication, is prohibited. Interested parties must apply directly to Random House, Inc. for permission.

Caroline Bunker Rosdahl and Mary T. Kowalski. Excerpt from *Textbook of Basic Nursing*, 9th ed. Copyright © 2008 Wolters Kluwer Health: Lippincott Williams & Wilkins.

Amy Tan. "Fish Cheeks." First appeared in *Seventeen* magazine. Reprinted by permission of the author and the Sandra Dijkstra Literary Agency.

Mark Twain. "Two Ways of Seeing a River." From *Life on the Mississippi*.

Commander Kristen Ziman. "Bad Attitudes and Glowworms." Originally appeared in the *Sun-Times Beacon News*, May 8, 2011. Reprinted by permission of the author.

Photo/Art Credits

Page 4: Courtesy of Mark DiMassimo, DiMassimo Goldstein, Tappening.

Index

example or explanation at beginning of, 181–82
gerund (-ing verbs) fragments, 179–80
infinitive (to + verb) fragments, 180–81
prepositional phrase fragments, 177–78
Frazier, Ian, "How to Operate a Shower Curtain," 104–6
Freewriting, topic, exploring, 26
Fused sentences
correcting, 186
defined, 183

G

Garcia, Christina, "Spanglish," 127–29
Gender of pronouns
pronoun agreement with, 205, 209
sexist language, avoiding, 206–7, 223
Gerunds (-ing verbs)
in fragments, 179–80
helping verbs with, 173
in misplaced modifiers, 215
sentence variety, use for, 219
"Gifts from the Heart" (Palmer), 80
good, comparative and superlative forms, 214
Google, topic, exploring with search, 28
Graham, Jeremy, "Becoming a Community Leader," 102–3
Grammar, errors in sentences. See Sentence errors
Guiding questions, for critical reading, 5

H

had. See also have, forms of
as helping verb, 173
in past-perfect tense, 202
hardly, as misplaced modifier, 215

has. See also have, forms of
as helping verb, 173
in present-perfect tense, 202
have, forms of
as helping verb, 173
in past participle, 198–202
past-perfect tense, 202
past tense of, 199
present-perfect tense, 202
present tense of, 189
subject-verb agreement with, 189–90
he
as subject pronoun, 208
subject-verb agreement with, 188–90
Headings, and critical reading, 5
Head note, and critical reading, 5
Helping verbs
functions of, 173
and -ing verb forms, 173
list of, 173
and past participles, 201–2
her
as object pronoun, 208
as possessive pronoun, 208
pronoun agreement with, 205
here, subject-verb agreement, 195
Hijuelos, Oscar, "Memories of New York City Snow," 93–95
him, as object pronoun, 208
his
as possessive pronoun, 208
pronoun agreement with, 205
sexist language, avoiding, 206–7, 223
Holidays, capitalization of, 237
how is, in writing assignment, 110
"How to Operate a Shower Curtain" (Frazier), 104–6
Hyde, Celia, police report by, 91–92
Hyphen, 235
Hyphenated words, 235

I
I
versus me, 208, 210
as subject pronoun, 208, 209
subject-verb agreement with, 188–90
Ibrahim, Said, "Eyeglasses vs. Laser Surgery: Benefits and Drawbacks," 139
Idea generation, in writing process, 20
identify, in writing assignment, 130, 154
-i changing to -y, for comparative/superlative forms, 213
Illustration, 73–85
basics of, 73–74
concluding sentences/conclusion in, 76–77
defined, 73
example readings, to read and analyze, 78–83
examples in, 76–77
main point in, 75, 76
order of importance organization, 78
paragraphs versus essays, 76–77
purpose for writing, 73–74
support points/supporting details in, 75–76
thesis statement in, 75–77
topic sentence in, 75, 76–77
writing, 83–85
writing situations for, 74, 83
Importance, order of. See Order of importance
"Importance of Advance Directives, The" (Melancon), 162–63
in, use, ESL writers, 170
Incomplete sentences. See Fragments
Incomplete thought, 173–74
Indefinite pronouns, 204–7
functions of, 206
list of, 194, 204–5
pronoun agreement with, 206–7

Four Basics of Good Writing

1 It achieves the writer's purpose.

2 It considers the readers (the audience).

3 It includes a main point.

4 It has details that support the main point.

2PR The Critical Reading Process

Preview the reading.

Read the piece, finding the main point and support.

Pause to think during reading. Ask yourself questions about what you are reading. Imagine that you are talking to the author.

Review the reading, your notes, and your questions. Build your vocabulary by looking up any unfamiliar words.